The Chicago Architectural Journal 8

• 10th Anniversary Edition •

RIZZOLI
NEW YORK

CATALOGVE OF THE TENTH ANNVAL EXHIBITION OF THE Chicago Architectvral Clvb at the Art Institvte

MDCCCXCVII

Cover for the *Catalog of the Tenth Annual Exhibition of the Chicago Architectural Club at the Art Institute* (1897)

Contents

The Chicago Architectural Journal
Compiled annually by the
Chicago Architectural Club

Editors
Deborah Doyle
Kevin Harrington
Anders Nereim

Design
Deborah Doyle

Production
Doyle & Ohle
Architects, Inc.

Editorial Assistant
Rachel Garbow

Editorial Committee
Michael Lustig
Janet Rogatz
Cynthia Weese

Board of Directors
Robert Bruegmann
Neil Frankel
Kevin Harrington, *President*
Linda Krause
Andrew Metter
Kathryn Quinn, *Treasurer*
Sidney Robinson
Kenneth Schroeder
Cynthia Weese, *Past President*
Stephen Wierzbowski

The Chicago Architectural Journal
4 West Burton Place
Chicago, Illinois 60610

First published in the United States of
America in 1989 by Rizzoli International
Publication, Inc.
300 Park Avenue South
New York, New York 10010

ISBN: 0-8478-5494-9

Dedication: to Carter H. Manny, Jr.

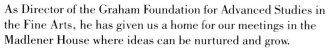

As Director of the Graham Foundation for Advanced Studies in the Fine Arts, he has given us a home for our meetings in the Madlener House where ideas can be nurtured and grow.

As former President of the Chicago Architectural Club, he has helped us see that order is preferable to chaos in a voluntary association whose members often march to different drummers.

As colleague and friend he makes clear everyday that he wears lightly his mantle of honor and integrity, characterized by a firm handshake, a light step and a warm smile.

Yet his service to the Club is only one of his many contributions. Repeatedly his role in directing the Graham Foundation has made a crucial difference in identifying and supporting the best and most promising new work in architecture and related disciplines. In the library of the Madlener House one encounters some of the most important books in the field world wide, and all of them have been supported by the Graham Foundation. He has sought out and found people of promise, especially young people whose work might not have been recognized otherwise. His greatest gift may be this ability to recognize the talents of others and encourage them in their work. Many recipients of his support, now among the leaders of their professions, have said that the help of the Graham Foundation has made a crucial difference in shaping their careers and contributions to their community.

We look forward to his continued friendship, leadership, guidance, encouragement and advice, and we shall strive to be worthy of his trust.

In celebrating the 10th Anniversary of the refounding of the Chicago Architectural Club we find ourselves violating Satchel Paige's advice, "Don't look back, something may be gaining on you." Our Janus-like behavior has characterized the club in its present era, whether we are glancing in the rear view mirror to be certain our past is really receding in the distance as we speed purposefully into the future, or whether we look over our shoulder as we muse about the present, and its complex relation to past and future.

Nearly every previous issue of the *Chicago Architectural Journal* has paired the current work of members with considerations of prior Chicago architects, fleshing out the history and tradition of this place. We have made such a comparison because we believe that past work still has much to teach us, and we know that our own work must stand up to that of our predecessors. We also know that whether or not the first and second Chicago Schools were as monolithic or disparate as various students have claimed, we must stick to our own home work if we ever hope to receive a passing grade.

Chicago is filled with the monuments of giants, and we are never sure, late at night, whether the sounds we hear are echoes of their approbation, or the approaching gale as they prepare to blow us off their shoulders as unworthy to stand there and consider the horizon.

Kevin Harrington

5

Introduction

Critic with [tongue in] Cheek Walks Plank

Being asked to summarize the work of the last 10 years of members of the Chicago Architectural Club is nothing worse than a certain death sentence. To make at this point anything resembling a judgmental assessment, anything categorical, is akin to walking the plank, or at a minimum, risking ridicule. So I look at this as an opportunity to learn from the recent past, and to make a few observations, but not to interpret events. As Paul Gapp said at an Architectural Club meeting in January 1984, "The intensity of the search for real meaning in architecture intrigues me. Why don't we just cool out and let the historians figure it out two centuries from now." At the same meeting the architecture critic of the *Chicago Tribune* opined on the state of architecture in the city of big shoulders. He called much of the work "New Mainstream," a term I scoffed at then and still consider so much bunk. Not only was there no prevailing current other than pluralism, but if something is "prevailing" (see *Webster*), how can it be new? It is useful to recall Gapp's term now, however, if only to emphasize its negative side: prevailing meaning the norm, the usual, and my interpretation, the mundane — The New Mundane.

This "New Mundane" was the dreadfully depressing summation I came to after rereading the previous volumes of the *Chicago Architectural Journal*. For several issues running, The New Mundane, also known as More of the Same, seemed an appropriate assessment of much of the work. This was particularly true of the commercial work, of which Tannys Langdon wrote in Volume 5: "[in] trying to be more interesting somehow we've managed to take dull elements and put them together in strange ways."

The primary missing ingredient, with few exceptions, was spirit. Most of the work emanating from the Hammond Beeby and Babka office — Jim Hammond, Tom Beeby, John Syvertsen, Tannys Langdon and John Clark — was infused with an ethereal quality that appealed to human sensibilities. It was cause for contemplation. But the machined forms of projects such as the Hollister Headquarters by Gerry Horn or the Federal Plaza in Milwaukee by Wojciech Madeyski, while competent — even beautiful in Horn's case — only briefly held the mind.

The work in Volume 1 of the *Journal* clearly represented a Chicago without an architectural direction. Not that it is necessary, simply because we live in a city with a history of architects like John Root, Daniel Burnham, and Mies van der Rohe, to have a mentor who shows us the way. But the lack of a

rigorous discipline or investigation — the void created since Walter Netsch retired field theory, Harry Weese stopped reshaping the lakefront, and Bertrand Goldberg moved south of the river — have left little for the critic to sink her teeth into.

Instead of construction, we talk about deconstruction, which appears to deconstruct even before we can get a bite of it. Contextualism is such an old saw that it's more interesting to find a non-contextual building these days. Avant garde ideas are on view at the Art Institute of Chicago, courtesy of the French! We seem to be on an architectural merry-go-round, and no one's been able to catch the brass ring, unless being on the cover of *GQ* or being named "one to watch" by *Esquire* certifies one as an Architect. So where are we? This is best assessed in Volumes 6 and 7, where Stanley Tigerman, the closest we come to intellectual leadership in Chicago, returns to the grid in the Formica showroom at the Mart and in a private home in Springfield, Illinois. Is the irreparable wound healing? Or is the grid an armature against the world? Or is it a maze?

To Tigerman's credit, the level of discussion about architecture has risen to a considerably more audible, if not higher, plane since he played an important role in forming the second Chicago Architectural Club. How this has translated into building architecture, however, is not yet evident. The essence of soul, spirit, and spirituality is still lacking in much that is built today, outranked by the clank of hard cash that is responsible for the crop of high-rises being cultivated in the Loop and, more alarmingly, on North Michigan Avenue. The Romance of scraping the sky has stayed with us, but unfortunately, the profit-driven formulas for high-rises have stayed too.

As the home of the skyscraper — or not the home, as Carl Condit now says — Chicago has a fascinating history of building. It is still imperative to look at Skidmore, Owings and Merrill, in particular the work of Adrian Smith and Joseph Gonzalez, to find the "state of the art" in high rise design today. And it's a pitiful stylistic issue that comes out of the investigation. How Smith went from the slickly gridded Olympia Centre (which with its bulge has all the visual stability of aspic) to the gussied-up 225 West Washington might as well be explained as bad advice from Ann Landers. Then along come the AT&T and NBC buildings in Chicago, not to mention Rowes Wharf or 110-120 Tremont Street in Boston, and Smith appears to be making a quilt of historicist proportions. Gonzalez, too, has consistently become more historicist, moving away from the punched window wall of a basically modern office building for Stamford, Connecticut, to an articulated curtainwall of travertine, glass, and steel for City Center in Philadelphia. The latter is topped with two lanterns. Should this be viewed as a scheme half as bright as Kohn Pedersen Fox's 900 North Michigan Avenue?

There has been a consistent exploration of form and materials at the office of Murphy/Jahn. Philip Castillo's 362 West Street in Durban, South Africa, is a replay of Helmut Jahn's spiralling Humana competition entry and a precursor of Jahn's Columbus Circle scheme for New York City. The octagonal tower with a crown-like top that Jahn first published as Wilshire Boulevard in 1983 shows up time and again under the names of other firm members: Martin Wolf's 9th and Figueroa Tower, Castillo's 52nd and Broadway proposal, and his Buero Center Nibelungenplatz, where the form is echoed on the oval roof piece. It's visually compelling, but no one is talking about the efficiency or lack thereof of the floor plate or the construction. There is a lot left untold in the architecture, and in the untelling, a seeming lack of architectural development.

More intriguing is the work of John Lahey at Solomon, Cordwell, Buenz, a firm that's been quietly working away with some substantial commissions, but bedazzling no one with style. Lahey seems to be finding his stride and designing singular buildings, notably the Kennedy Three tower for Milwaukee. The vertical telescoping sections and balancing acts on the entry elevation add a gravity-defying character that is both visual and structural. Also noteworthy are Ralph Johnson's explorations of symmetry. His office building and hotel complex on the Chicago River is a trio of setback towers with a crispness that has about it a sense of sureness, reinforced by symmetry. It is a long way from the undulating wall and asymmetric form of Johnson's Ingalls Memorial Hospital Human Resources Center in Harvey.

Who has influenced the changes in these architects designs? It could just as well have been Dan Rather or George Bush as Aldo Rossi or Robert Venturi. More likely it is the developers. The depth of their pockets determines what's built, and they are sensitive to the tides of change, particularly the rip-tides of fashion, when it comes to making a buck.

Personal explorations might better be tracked in the single family house, where it is easier to experiment with form and content, and far more difficult to decipher a trend. Ken

Schroeder has almost single-handedly kept alive the postmodern cutout facade, to the point where it may become Chicago's vernacular of the 80's. The vernacular of the farm also crops up a number of times. Larry Booth's Elkus Compound in Iowa is a cultured interpretation of the utilitarian farm building, and Tom Beeby's Shutack House is composed of barnyard elements. Less successful are John Clark's recent incorporations of silo and milk can forms, which lack both the serious execution and the romanticism of his earlier work.

Then there is the striking resolve of Ron Krueck and Keith Olsen, and Darcy Bonner and Scott Himmel, who are developing through their sculptural use of glass and steel a personal vocabulary of forms and materials. The luxuriousness of their molded interior spaces offsets the chilling idea of literally living in a machine. The elevations of Bonner's Eagle Residence in Dallas (fig. 1) are collages, but based on a module that roots the work in a certain logic.

Tannys Langdon has maintained an interest in the fictional, and her crowning achievement to date is the Hole-in-the-Wall-Gang Camp. This fictional little town of timber and log construction is worlds apart from Krueck and Olsen's glass and steel houses, but their commonality is twofold. Each represents a personal quest, a honing of personal sensibilities, and neither speaks to any particular Chicago tradition other than craftsmanship.

The closest we come to approximating a Chicago tradition is at the office of Ben and Cynthia Weese, who at times remind me of Marion Mahoney and Walter Burley Griffin. Cynthia's houses have an Arts and Crafts vernacular of the prairie that roots them to their sites. Ben's churches have a timeless quality and a natural spirituality that in so many other contemporary religious buildings seem forced. They are apparently more interested in making beautiful, habitable buildings, than they are caught up in the theoretical exercises that Stanley Tigerman, for one, puts himself through to come up with a piece of architecture.

Perhaps the link that ties all of these architects and their work to Chicago is the grid, something like the net the city casts out to knit together a region. Whether laid on the land or pulled up into three dimensional form, it provides a framework for movement and experimentation. This is obvious in Tigerman's elaborate manipulation of the grid in his apartment building at Fukuoka, Japan (fig. 2), and in the work of Bruce Graham, who

7

only in the last ten years would be considered in the same breath as Tigerman.

Graham, in an interview upon the 50th anniversary of SOM, said of his Bishopsgate project in London that he wanted the British to know it was a building by a Chicago architect.[1] What Graham chose to design was not the Chicago of the Inland Steel Building. Rather, it is the work of a man who has taken a new look at the city around him and found a different vocabulary, one more adaptable to the individual city. On cursory inspection the bedecked Bishopsgate is a far cry from the pristine, structural geometry of Perimeter Center in Atlanta, but in fact both buildings are about the grid, its literal meaning and its cloaked presence.

At that January 1984 meeting of the Chicago Architectural Club, Gapp, Stuart Cohen, and Bruce Graham were asked to hash out representation and/or/versus abstraction in architecture. "I don't take a position where we have one form of architecture versus another," Graham said. Perhaps it is this seamless quality of building, a revisionist process that constantly alters our perceptions, that best characterizes the overall work of the Architectural Club. Is it necessary to argue the fine points of abstraction over representation when abstraction is just another form of representation?

When Graham steps down from SOM this year, so goes the semblance of leadership — of the kind that builds — in Chicago's architectural community. The mantle may not go to another SOM partner. It may go to the next generation, perhaps to someone whose sensibility returns the soul to architecture. This kind of sensibility is already evident in the work of Andrew Metter and Dan Wheeler: in the dignity offered to the workers by Metter's handsome public works facilities (fig. 3), and in the simplicity of Wheeler's single room house addition (fig. 4), where a section reminiscent of Louis Kahn suggests a return to spirituality. But as I noted at the beginning, we should let the historians figure it out two centuries from now.

Cynthia C. Davidson

Cynthia C. Davidson has been the editor of Inland Architect *magazine since 1983, and last year she was awarded a Loeb Fellowship in Advanced Environmental Studies at Harvard University's Graduate School of Design.*

1. "An Interview with Bruce Graham," *Inland Architect*, March/April 1987

8

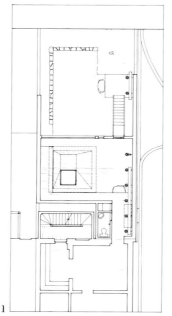

1

2

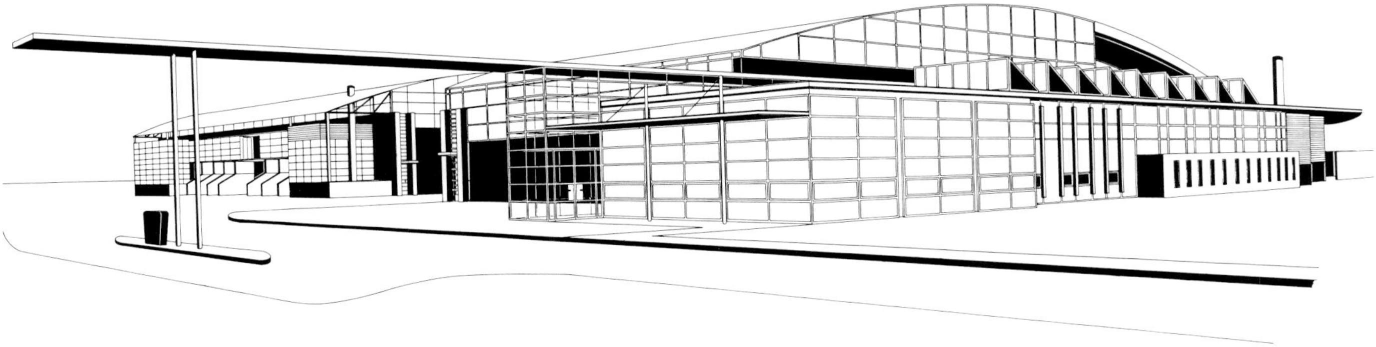

4

Fig . 1: Eagle residence, Dallas Texas, by Bonner and Himmel

Fig . 2: Apartment Building in Fukouka, Japan by Tigerman McCurry

*Fig . 3: Bloomingdale Public Works Building, by Perkins and Will,
with Andrew Metter as designer*

*Fig . 4: Single Room House Addition Project in Chicago by Daniel
Wheeler Architects*

Linking the headstone of the first Chicago Architectural Club to the cornerstone of the second one, I imagine a bridge, for a tunnel would only expose the sediments of events between the 20's and the 80's. Standing up here at the crown of the arch you can look all around, but you can also get lost in the fog. Whether this is a report of clear sightings or foggy apparitions remains to be seen.

The Chicago Architectural Club is intimately bound up with the evolution of the professions in general. The late 19th century saw a proliferation of groups who performed specialized services that required advanced education. These professionals saw themselves as an important force in the maturing nation. They began assuming some of the leadership roles which traditionally had been found in agriculture, manufacturing and trade groups. When managing, writing, and designing achieved more cultural prominence, their associated specialized intellectual and cultural activities also became more important.

Professional clubs helped identify these new roles to their members, and to society at large. It was self-promotion, pure and simple. Of course there were educational goals, but they were also tied up in solidifying a group's social and economic position. It all seemed, and generally was, an innocent activity.

Today, many things have changed, but not everything. The profession is still concerned with its stature. It still makes sense to provide educational programs. In the decades since the 20's, the profession of architecture has been successful, and along with other professions has established itself in the public consciousness. But today as we assert a claim of high-

minded concern for the best interests of everyone, it can be challenged by any aggressive individual who counters: "Says who?" The missing force is the spur of passionate discussion and persuasion. We benefited from the redistribution of power 80 years ago, but we fear that those gains have been lost as further redistribution has left us with no leadership position at all.

Is the new Chicago Architectural Club an expression of nostalgia for a more innocent time? Is it simply a rear-guard action to preserve distinctiveness by seeming exclusive and sophisticated? Or is it just a social place to relax into arcane jargon after a hard day of failing to make clients understand?

I think it is more complex than that. Architects today are suffering from an unintended consequence of modernist morality. Modernism tried to eradicate an architecture that it characterized as nothing but rhetorical flourishes. Eclecticism had no heart, only a painted face. The modernist rallying cry was to get back to basics; to necessities of function, materials, changing technology and perception. The inflammatory attacks at the beginning of the century were designed not to convince but to exact submission. If you believe that history will inevitably overtake the opposition, there is no reason to make an effort to understand their errors. Successful rhetoric, however, succeeds in part by recognizing where the opposition is, and why it is there. Modernists had no need of rhetoric.

Having thrown out rhetoric, we watched as the ranks of modernism splintered, with no way of considering differences even among partisans. When the second Chicago Architectural Club was established, modernist dogma had become so

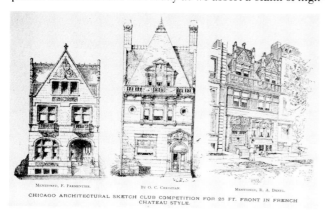

Fig. 1: Winners of the "Chicago Architectural Sketch Club Competition for a 25 Ft. Front in the French Chateau Style,"

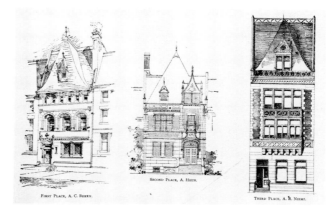

from Inland Architect and News Record *XIII no. 3 (March 1889)*

10

permissive that arrogance no longer had any function. All we are left with is a suffocating tolerance spread around in the name of good manners. Based on the way we treated the real opposition, we are afraid that we will come to blows with our colleagues. We need to argue and convince and we cannot. Our professional education avoids rhetoric like the plague. We lament that recent graduates cannot write, but we don't really believe it's useful for anything besides recording meeting notes or confirming a harried telephone conversation with a polite letter.

Without a tradition of rhetoric, we let people say their piece about architecture, and keep our responses to ourselves. Passion cannot be permitted an outlet in rebuttal. Because we have not practiced rhetoric, we cannot use it. Without it we can't reach any agreement about the revitalization of our cities except for their destruction and rebuilding. The cities attest to our mastery of that tactic. If this is all we bring to the discussion of architecture, the only hope for a vital architectural community lies in a perpetual revolution of the third, fourth and fifth Chicago Architectural Clubs.

That is, unless we learn to use rhetoric to convince, to discuss, to engage in energetic exchanges about architecture. Of course there must be something significant to talk about. The current predominance of surfaces represented by photography over the multifaceted presence of architecture is often cited as proof that representations like words are at best fluff and at worst sinister distractions from the real thing. For those discouraged by what only looks like too much rhetoric, the solution lies in a return to the days when architects indicated the truth by mutely pointing at their buildings. If rhetoric badly exercised is foolishness, no rhetoric at all is sheer cussedness.

If any city should be a challenging place to practice architecture, Chicago is it. But the very success of a certain kind of modernism rendered architecture helpless to go forward. The second Chicago Architectural Club could be the place for us to face this challenge, but we would have to come to terms with an intimidating body of work from the past. If we persist in thinking about architecture as either triumph or submission, we will be unable to engage our past, let alone our present, in a critical dialogue. Acquiring new rhetorical skills is not easy, particularly when they were once thought to be so contaminated, but learning to clarify and recompose differences will expose new alternatives and save us from a terminal state of tolerance. By entertaining and challenging marginal propositions we can make Chicago's architecture vital once again.

11

Sidney K. Robinson

An architect and historian with degrees from Columbia and Michigan, he teaches at the University of Illinois at Chicago. He has published works on the Prairie School, Frank Lloyd Wright, and Alden Dow, and recently sent to press a book entitled Essays on the Picturesque.

Fig. 2: Winners of the Chicago Townhouse Exhibition at the Graham Foundation, Chicago, May, 1978. From left to right: James Goettsch, Deborah Doyle, Anders Nereim, Joseph Poli, Peter Pran, Robert Fugman, Frederick Read, and Steven Gross.

"But We Are Not in France":
Early Competitions from the Chicago Architectural
Sketch Club

One of the earliest clubs for architectural draftsmen, the Chicago Architectural Sketch Club was established in 1885 to provide young draftsmen with exhibitions and frequent competitions, so they could educate themselves in the functional, artistic, and theoretical aspects of the practice of architecture and the applied arts.[1] The club attracted the support of Chicago's practicing architects, who were reforming the standards and identity of their profession. In an article at the end of the Chicago club's first decade, architect P. B. Wight praised the ink sketches (Fig. 1), renderings, and prize-winning competition designs in the club's eighth annual exhibition.[2] While he commended the advanced work executed by American architects, influenced by the competition standards of the Ecole des Beaux-Arts, Wight stated, "But we are not in France." He reminded his readers of the conditions separating American architects and draftsmen from their colleagues in Paris. Since the 1880s, Wight and his colleagues had sought to remedy the underrated professional status of the architect and the unguided quality of architectural education.

The annual exhibitions and frequent competitions of the Chicago Architectural Sketch Club influenced the daily practice and professional goals of local draftsmen and architects. These contests varied in building type, program, material, jury membership, and patronage because of the shifting demands of the club's membership and an increasingly informed audience of contractors, manufacturers, and building owners. Competitions not only strengthened draftsmen's design practices, but also raised professional standards and advised public taste in matters of civic, commercial, and domestic architecture. Whether local or national, these competitions fostered the Chicago Architectural Sketch Club's objective: "the advancement and improvement of its members in all matters pertaining to architecture."[3] As early as March 1889,

architect George Beaumont could boast of the club's high standards to the Illinois State Association of Architects:

> The monthly competitions in designing have produced some really good work and show what rapid strides have been made by many of the members, not only in the conception and general working out of the subjects given but in the rendering of the drawings, particularly in watercolors. This is the club's forte . . .[4]

Throughout the period ending with the Tenth Annual Exhibition in 1897, the club prospered from the wide support of Chicago's practicing architects, who served as club officers or competition judges in their efforts to teach the profession to draftsmen.

Early on, the club organized several different types of architectural competitions. Initially, these competitions were open only to club members, to foster discussion among practicing architects and draftsmen. The club's earliest competitions in 1885 were initiated and supported by groups or individuals representing building material manufacturers and suppliers.[5] In February 1885 Henry Lord Gay, founding editor of *Building Budget* arranged a design competition for a hall mantle. The exhibition and publication of winning mantel designs attracted at least two audiences: clients who were then commissioning large residences, and practicing Chicago architects. The drawings might also advance a draftsman's career, by attracting attention and possible employment in the leading architect's offices.

Before long, the club's increased membership and growing impact on the architectural profession permitted them to initiate monthly competitions.[6] An important subject announced at least three times was the city house front (see page 10). Adjudicating committee member John Root reported

12

1

2

to the July 1, 1889 club meeting the winners of a "Competition for 25 Ft Front in French Chateau Style." Beyond reflecting the building type's popularity among developers, such a competition fostered consistent projects to enhance the sketch club's educational goals.

Club officers also diversified the subjects for club competitions to broaden the design experience of young draftsmen before they became practicing architects. Competition subjects were often inspired by new recreational or transportation needs. An 1894 club competition for a road house for cyclists addressed a relatively new building type brought about by the popularity of the bicycle (Fig. 2). The program provided cyclists with an informal building in the countryside, equipped with a kitchen, dining room, ladies parlor, and upstairs sleeping rooms. Presenting a picturesque view that only hints at materials in seemingly quickly-sketched lines, this winning drawing suggested the pleasurable recreation associated with bicycle-riding in the countryside. Club competitions provided opportunities for draftsmen to learn design strategies from one another, and design standards from the practicing architects who selected the winners.

In July 1889, the Chicago Architectural Sketch Club announced two new competitions through *Inland Architect*. The Phimister Medal Competition and the Robert Clark Prize Competition were gifts from private citizens who wished to direct national attention to the Chicago club's efforts to advance the training of American architectural draftsmen. These gifts immediately elevated the club's professional significance to a national level and insured its prominence as a decisive and guiding architectural organization. The Phimister Competition never attracted the same response as the Robert Clark Medal Competition, which elicited entries from all over the country for more than a decade.

The purpose of the Clark Prize Competition was to aid "the development of architectural design and draftsmanship in this country."[7] The competition was open to American draftsmen under thirty years of age who were not practicing architects. They were not allowed to collaborate. *Inland Architect* published official competition circulars and codes, as well as subsequent reports that highlighted both the merits and problems of the top entries. A changing adjudicating committee awarded a silver and a gold medal to successful

3

contestants. Each year, American draftsmen were invited by the Clark Prize committee to propose plans and elevations to suit a specific program and building type. These usually were public buildings, such as railroad terminals, clubs, schools, and park buildings. The competition's organization, building types, selection process, and winning designs ably summarize the contemporary concerns of draftsmen, architects, patrons, and public. The authoritative judgment and commentary from Chicago architects permitted the club to embody for the profession and the public the essential design components of modern American architecture.

The first Clark Prize Competition established the national competition's methods and organization. The problem asked draftsmen to design an apartment house for tenants of moderate means, reflecting the widespread efforts to improve living conditions for masses in need of healthy shelter. Draftsmen were required to submit plans of the basement, first and second stories, one elevation and one perspective, all in India-ink line drawings. The five-member adjudicating committee for the

1889 Clark Prize consisted of architects Dankmar Adler (Chair), Henry Ives Cobb, N. Clifford Ricker, Samuel A. Treat, and sculptor Lorado Taft. Several ballots determined the different medal winners. The annual Clark Prize Competition and the club's agenda of regular competitions secured for the club and Chicago's practicing architects an influential role throughout the following years of pivotal change in domestic, civic, and commercial architecture.

During the 1890s, larger annual exhibitions and illustrated exhibition catalogs were initiated, and together these made the club's cycle of competitions even more significant to the profession and especially to the public. The Clark Medal competitions were often highlighted in the club's annual exhibitions and illustrated catalogs. The catalogs even prompted a regular club competition to design the cover (see frontispiece). In contrast to the club's first competitions, devoted often to detail or interior renderings for an audience consisting largely of builders and material manufacturers, later Clark Prize Competitions and regular club competitions

4

14

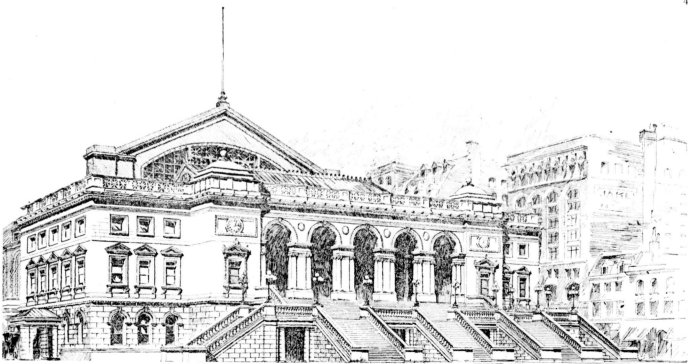

focused on public building programs for a large professional audience of practicing architects and urban planners. By 1894, the architectural profession had transformed the earlier "sketch club project" into the "architectural event of the year."[8]

Hundreds of entries from all over the country were screened by Juries of Admission for architecture and decoration, decorative subjects, and sculpture, for the club's seventh annual exhibition of 1894. Local and national competitions from other cities were frequently exhibited at the annual exhibitions, providing Chicago's draftsmen and architects with an ideal opportunity to learn.[9] The Chicago Architectural Club's Clark Medal Competition continued to shape architectural design standards, to mold how architects thought about their profession, and to establish high standards for instructive architectural criticism.

The club's Fifth Annual (1893) Robert Clark Medal Competition for an elevated railroad terminal station is notable especially for the critical discourse among practicing architects, draftsmen, and the public. Each group was learning to articulate for a different audience what constituted successful architectural planning and in this way competitions

5

15

helped to educate diverse viewers. Plans and entries were exhibited first at the club's annual banquet in November, 1893 and *Inland Architect* published the names of all competitors, the prize winners, and a lengthy committee report. The Adjudicating Committee including W. L. B. Jenny (Chair), S. A. Treat, Charles A. Coolidge, Lorado Taft, and D. H. Burnham, wrote general criticisms on the entire group, and detailed criticisms of individual projects that were awarded medals or honorable mention. [10] The report reveals that the judges expected the draftsmen to satisfy three major conditions in their plan: ample interior light, easy movement of many people from the street to the trains, and clear separation of people entering and exiting the building. In general, the committee found no design which was superior to all others in both plan and elevation. Many designs were rejected when they failed to meet these practical requirements for moving large numbers of people. It did not matter that these projects were not meant to be built. Competitions were especially useful as teaching devices because they provided students with typical programs they would encounter as practicing architects.

Directing their readers' attention to specific award-winning entries, the committee described their perceived merit and faults, and recommended improvements in plan or elevation. Benjamin W. Trunk's Bronze Medal Design (Fig. 3) was praised for its effective plan, but the jury was "greatly confused by the too prominent rendering of the mosaic." Although Trunk's drawing technique was praised, the building's style was faulted as "adapted to certain localities only." From Chicago, Edward Garden's First Honorable Mention Design (Fig. 4) was faulted for the splintered arrangement of stairs that give "an unquiet feeling" to the exterior, and for the unnecessary importance given to the train shed over the passenger terminal. Although not awarded a prize, John Richmond's entry was praised for its superb drawing, and was kept by the committee for hanging in the club rooms (Fig. 5).

Together these comments and the prizes suggest the committee's bias toward rationally planned buildings. Through important competitions, the club provided an instructive and diversified forum for Chicago architects and draftsmen to debate the merits and faults of Beaux-Arts training, as opposed to what they called more practical training. The annual exhibitions and competitions were central methods for fostering this debate. At the club's Seventh Annual Exhibition in May

1894, the railroad terminal drawings were exhibited in the Art Institute in spacious galleries, which significantly enlarged the audience that was addressed by the competitions and exhibitions. Testifying to the significance of this competition, at the 1894 annual exhibition the Chicago Architectural Sketch Club chose to represent its entire year's efforts solely with these entries to the 1893 Robert Clark Medal Competition.

The Sixth Annual Robert Clark Medal Competition (1894) demonstrated how competitions and their small exhibitions could foster professional ties between two important but separate architectural associations. The competition called in September 1894 for young draftsmen to design an Art Club in a Classic or Renaissance style, the building to be situated on a residence boulevard. [11] The project was judged by W. B. Mundie (Chair), Frank Lloyd Wright, and Irving K. Pond. This competition's related private exhibition turned into one of the club's most notable meetings, because it coincided with the 1895 American Institute of Architects Annual Convention in Chicago. [12] Many visiting architects and A. I. A. officers attended the club's meeting, and the evening concluded with the presentation of the Illinois Chapter A. I. A. Gold Medal, a

6

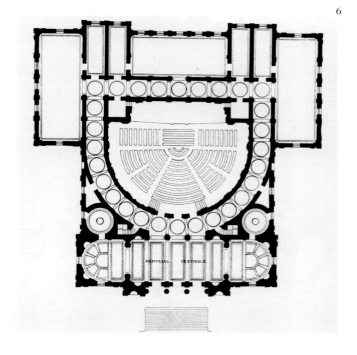

prominent separate competition which had consistently been part of the Chicago club's annual agenda.

The annual Gold Medal of the Illinois Chapter of the A.I.A. was offered exclusively to members of the Chicago club, and the prestigious competition was given particular focus the following Spring at the Eighth Annual Exhibition of 1895. The subject, "A Building Dedicated to the Study of Botany, Zoology and Mineralogy," was judged by Charles Frost, T.O. Frankel, and August Fiedler. The A.I.A. preferred Beaux-Arts classicism, and the Gold Medal was awarded to Elmer C. Jensen, whose plan (Fig. 6), elevation, and cross-section were reproduced in the annual exhibition catalog. The club also reproduced other notable competition drawings, including elevations by Hugh Garden (Fig. 7), Charles E. Birge (Fig. 8). The Gold Medal competition insured that Chicago draftsmen and architects would remain in contact with the A.I.A.'s methods and standards.

At the Chicago Architectural Club's Tenth Annual Exhibition in 1897, the Club again exhibited only the Robert Clark Medal Competition to represent its entire year's production. The subject was "a bath house for a small city, to be placed in the city park."[13] Judges Louis J. Millet, Charles Coolidge, and Jeremiah K. Cady awarded prizes to David Meyers of Boston (Fig. 9) and John F. Jackson of Buffalo. The club also displayed drawings from distant club competitions. Robert Clark, Henry Lord Gay, and D.G. Phimister, generous patrons who had established national and club competitions, were made honorary members on this occasion, recognizing their vision that architectural competitions would advance the draftsman's and architect's profession, and lead to progress in American architectural education.

Architectural sketch clubs set forth in the 1880s to improve the American draftsman's opportunities for education and advancement in the profession, to establish reliable methods of professional training and practice, and to generally raise the standards and public regard for the architectural profession. The Chicago Architectural Sketch Club maintained a regular agenda of national and local competitions to sustain these goals. Indeed, contemporaries might have argued that without competitions to expand and nurture the goals of draftsmen and architects, the Chicago Architectural Sketch Club would have failed its purposes.

7

· PRINCIPAL FACADE ·

+ A BVILDING DEVOTED TO THE STVDY OF BOTANY, ZOOLOGY AND MINERALOGY +

NOTES:

1. The club changed its name officially in 1895 to the Chicago Architectural Club. For other information on the club's history, see Wilbert R. Hasbrouck, "The Early Years of the Chicago Architectural Club," *Chicago Architectural Journal 1* (1981), pp. 7-14, and John Zukowsky, "The Chicago Architectural Club, 1895-1940," *Chicago Architectural Journal 2* (1982), pp. 170-74.

2. P.B. Wight, "Annual Exhibition of the Chicago Architectural Club," *Inland Architect and Building News 25 No. 5* (June 1895), pp. 47-50. The quoted sentence appears on page 49.

3. The club's constitution and by laws were published in *Inland Architect and Building News 5 Number 3* (April 1885), pp. 37-8. The journal's editor, Robert Craik McLean, encouraged the club's growing success by frequently publishing articles and drawings related to competitions, early history, and annual exhibitions.

4. The paper was published by McLean. See George Beaumont, "History and Development of the Chicago Architectural Sketch Club," *Inland Architect and News Record 13 Number 4* (April 1889), pp. 57-8.

5. Hasbrouck, p. 10.

6. Beaumont, p. 57.

7. "The Clark Prize Competition," *Inland Architect and News Record 13 Number 8* (July 1889), p. 103.

8. "Association Notes," *Inland Architect and News Record 23 Number 3* (April 1894), p. 34.

9. "Seventh Annual Exhibition, C.A.S.C.," *Inland Architect and News Record 23 Number 4* (May 1894), p. 38.

10. "Robert Clark Medal Competition," *Inland Architect and News Record 22 Number 5* (December 1893), pp. 46-7.

11. "Competition, Robert Clark Testimonial," *Inland Architect and News Record 24 Number 2* (September 1894), p. 17.

12. "Chicago Architectural Sketch Club," *Inland Architect and News Record 24 Number 6* (January 1895), p. 59.

13. *Catalog of the Tenth Annual Exhibition of the Chicago Architectural Club at the Art Institute* (1897), p. 16.

8

FIGURE CAPTIONS:

Fig. 1: *Pen sketch of T.O. Fraenkel from the* Catalogue of the Seventh Annual Exhibition of the Chicago Architectural Sketch Club (1894)

Fig. 2: *John Johnson's first place design for the "Chicago Sketch Club Competition for a Road House for Cyclists," from* Inland Architect and News Record *XXIV, no. 3 (September 1894)*

Fig. 3: *Ben W. Trunk's bronze medal design for "An Elevated Railroad Terminal Station," for the 1983 Robert Clark Competition, from the* Catalogue of the Seventh Annual Exhibition of the Chicago Architectural Sketch Club *(1894)*

Fig. 4: *Edward G. Garden's first honorable mention design for "An Elevated Railroad Terminal Station," for the 1893 Robert Clark Competition, from the* Catalogue of the Seventh Annual Exhibition of the Chicago Architectural Sketch Club *(1894)*

Fig. 5: *John Richmond's design for "An Elevated Railroad Terminal Station," for the 1893 Robert Clark Competition, from the* Catalogue of the Seventh Annual Exhibition of the Chicago Architectural Sketch Club *(1894)*

Fig. 6: *Elmer C. Jensen's prize-winning plan for "A Memorial Building Devoted to the Study of Botany, Zoology and Mineralogy," for the Illinois Chapter AIA Gold Medal Competition, from the* Catalogue of the Eighth Annual Exhibition of the Chicago Architectural Sketch Club (1895)

Fig. 7: *Hugh M.G. Garden's elevation of "A Memorial Building Devoted to the Study of Botany, Zoology and Mineralogy," for the Illinois Chapter AIA Gold Medal Competition, from the* Catalogue of the Eighth Annual Exhibition of the Chicago Architectural Sketch Club (1895)

Fig. 8: *Chas. E. Birge's elevation of "A Memorial Building Devoted to the Study of Botany, Zoology and Mineralogy," for the Illinois Chapter AIA Gold Medal Competition, from the* Catalogue of the Eighth Annual Exhibition of the Chicago Architectural Sketch Club (1895)

Fig. 9: *David J. Myers's gold medal plan for "A Bath House for a Small City," for the 1896 Robert Clark Competition, from the* Catalogue of the Tenth Annual Exhibition of the Chicago Architectural Sketch Club *(1897)*

Stephen Sennott

Stephen Sennott is a Ph.D. student at the University of Chicago with interests including the Arts and Crafts movement and the reaction of Chicago architects to the automobile. He has taught architectural history at the University of Illinois in Chicago.

19

9

Going for Baroque in Milwaukee

In the annals of urban planning, this anecdote about Le Corbusier's project for the 1922 *Salon d'Automne* might seem insignificant. The salon director had explained that the theme of the exhibition was urbanism, and asked if the architect would care to contribute a monumental fountain? Le Corbusier agreed, as long as he could design a contemporary city for three million people behind it. His audacious verbal and visual response aimed at nothing less than a complete re-ordering of urban design priorities. Fountains and other "ornaments" had little place in the functional, efficient, city of tomorrow.

So how do we explain a pair of monumental triumphal arches in the *Ville Contemporaine?* As elements on the main boulevard they reinforced the city's dominant axis, much the way the Arc du Carousel and Arc de Triomphe worked on the Champs Elysees. One could view these arches as part of a Parisian *"porte"* penchant. But stripped of specific commemorative references, and dissociated from historic precincts (not to mention revolutionary politics), Le Corbusier's arches became abstract objects whose only function was to mark the entrance to the city.

With postmodernism, the monument returned to the city, and the referential site-and-place-specific-gateway supplanted the de-valued modernist arch. Both the 1986 and 1987 Burnham Prize programs called for gateways. Many designs for enhancing downtown Milwaukee have incorporated this feature, the most recent being entries in the International City Design Competition (ICDC) sanctioned by the International Union of Architects (IUA), and sponsored by the School of Architecture and Urban Planning at the University of Wisconsin in Milwaukee (fig. 1).

The ICDC sought "credible visions" for improving Milwaukee. Though several of the visions were incredible, most of the entries were at least tenable. One popular "improvement" was a broad boulevard linking the Milwaukee River with Lake Michigan. The lakefront entrance to the boulevard was marked by monumental gateways, ranging from triumphal arches to matching set-back skyscrapers. Does this mean that Le Corbusier's vision of towers in the park has been replaced by 19th century urban set-pieces and models of *moderne*-ity? Yes and no.

Stylistically, the Milwaukee gateways are pre-modern, but the boulevard/gateway scheme transcends style. Despite its Machine Age rhetoric, Le Corbusier's Contemporary City preserved with a fetish the Baroque infatuation with order, hierarchy, and the monument terminating a triumphal way. This last feature was especially favored by 19th century planners. By giving our sanction to these Baroque elements we extend the Bernini-Haussmann-Le Corbusier line to the present. Though modernists and anti-modernists speak a different language, when it comes to urban design we can see that they share the same grammar, or rules imposed to standardize their use of forms. This grammar is so persistent that we might well wonder if change is possible, or even desirable.

As for the possible, the ICDC request for "credible" schemes reveals a bias for conventional designs. Credible means believable, even tending toward the familiar, in other words those forms legitimized by convention. This doesn't mean that all the ICDC entries were predictable or banal; far from it. But the winning designs leaned toward the pragmatic and customary, because the jurors acted in good faith, given the preference for credibility. But why not have varied award criteria with winning designs in different categories? Perhaps some architects might be rewarded for the quality of their critical thinking, or a planner might be cited for an innovative approach to the design process. A change in the grammar of urban planning is possible if we challenge the familiar assumptions.

But the possibility of change does not mean that change is necessarily desirable. So what if we can trace these gateway boulevards back to 17th century Rome? While many will argue that we must return to legitimizing authority, reliance on the past is always problematic. At best, Baroque schemes can still reveal a lack of imagination, and at worst they demand the total suppression of local conditions.

The ICDC winners illustrate this point. The program booklet included dozens of photos of the downtown area, revealing broad straight streets mainly bordered by low, widely spaced buildings. Milwaukee may be many things, but congested it is not. Indeed, the urban views were actually disturbing for their lack of people and cars. But this was no aberration. Save for rush hour and the inside of the Grand Avenue Mall, central Milwaukee looks about as lively it might really be after a high speed neutron event. The urban center does not need another boulevard, and certainly not one that ends in a superfluous gateway.

Gateways raise associations, and expectations of demarcation and commemoration. These gateways do neither. No one would pass through them, nor do they mark the confluence of Lake Michigan and the Milwaukee River. They hardly ask us to consider the physical act of entering the city, much less a political act of commemorating an event or place. They are empty gestures towards a past that is replicated but not questioned. As such, ironically, they actually become the abstract, reified objects that they were meant to replace.

These boulevard-gateway schemes reveal the triumph of cliche over both imagination and common sense. They are reminiscent of some well-publicized harbor designs for Chicago, despite significant differences in the two cities. And they surely defy common sense when we recall the European context of Baroque urban design. Versailles and Washington, D.C., aside, the grand boulevard was typically imposed on a densely-built medieval urban-fabric. The goal from Haussmann to Le Corbusier was *order*. Milwaukee isn't medieval, and it wasn't built densely. It is obsessively neat and ordered. Locked in its grid, the city is delimited, defined, and sectioned. What saves the plan from utter tedium are the subtle shifts and variations in the grid. The last thing Milwaukee needs is something that simply reinforces the grid.

Doubtless their proponents believed that the boulevards and gateways would connect disparate and under-appreciated features of the city such as the river and the lake. But Milwaukeeans already flock to the lakefront for its parks, public beaches, and a summer-long series of ethnic and cultural festivals. Activities along and on the river should prove similarly attractive, and there is already interest in developing river walks and river side markets. The waterways that border the urban core deserve the attention of municipal authorities, architects, planners, and the public. Insofar as this ICDC competition focuses that attention, it is worthwhile. But rigid, ill-conceived Baroque ensembles waste scarce revenues and diminish a sense of liveliness, spontaneity, and wonder. They suppress what is unique about a place. Saddest, they foster a complacent, even fearful, approach toward urban design.

Linda R. Krause

An architectural theorist and historian, Linda Krause teaches at the University of Wisconsin at Milwaukee. Her interests range from Victorian urban planning to the history of architectural theory.

Fig. 1: Proposed "Grand Boulevard" for Milwaukee, by Toshio Tsushimi and Jan Zandenkieboom, Architects.

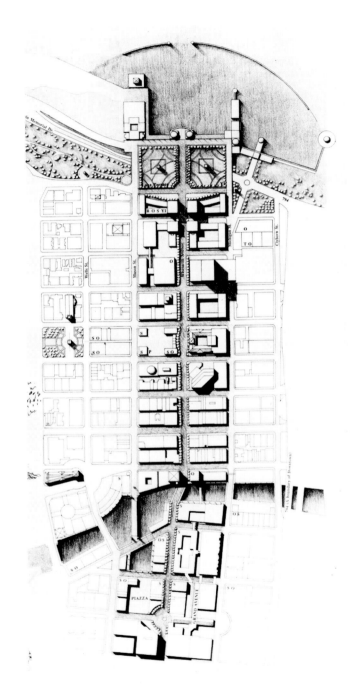

21

Courtesy of the School of Architecture and Urban Planning, University of Wisconsin at Milwaukee.

Barcelona's Best

The city of Barcelona is now undertaking its most important planning project of the century. Traditionally Barcelona's Mediterranean coastline has been used exclusively for industrial rather than recreational purposes, and it was isolated from the rest of the city by railroad tracks. Today that industrial coastline is being transformed into the city's only extended recreational area on the Mediterranean Sea, a development inspired by planning for the 1992 Olympic Games.

In order to accommodate the Olympics, the local, regional, and national governments of Barcelona and Spain have funded sports stadia, offices, housing, etc. on several sites around the city. Buildings to be constructed include a 200,000-seat domed stadium by Arata Isozaki, with references to a Japanese temple; the renovation of an existing 70,000-seat stadium originally built for the International Exposition of 1929; and a Press Center designed by Ricardo Bofill, which will be used by a local university after the Olympics. The construction of a village to house the athletes and press and the contiguous transformation of one kilometer of coastline will be the most important residuals to emerge from the Olympic planning.

There have been many previous proposals to reclaim this coastline for nonindustrial development, the first of which was drawn up in the early 19th century. However, the development of the industrial port and the expansion of the railway precluded any non-industrial use until today. The current plan was drawn up by an Olympic Planning Committee that studied the features of Barcelona and designated the Olympic sites so they could be well integrated into the fabric of the city, fulfilling larger planning needs. It was then developed by the architectural team of Martorell, Bohigas, Mackay, and Puigdomenech.

Reminiscent of the 1909 Plan of Chicago, the coastline reclamation will include two large beaches, two breakwaters at the ports of Barceloneta and Bogatell, and a harbor for the mooring of small boats. In addition, a large park will connect the Olympic Village to the beachfront, and the railroad tracks will be rerouted so they no longer separate the land from the sea. Commissions for the buildings in the Olympic Village will be given to twenty Barcelona architects who have won annual design awards from Spain's equivalent of the American Institute of Architects. Plans also include the construction of two high-rises, one designed by Bruce Graham for Skidmore, Owings and Merrill in Chicago. Following the Olympics, the area will become Barcelona's newest residential area. Together the new housing and waterfront will be significant residuals for Barcelona, long after another city has accepted the Olympic torch.

1

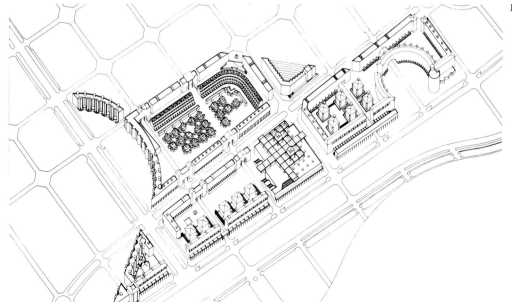

Fig. 1: Axonometric of the residential zone set aside for the Olympic Village

Fig. 2: Plan of the development

Pauline Saliga

Pauline Saliga is Assistant Curator in the Department of Architecture at The Art Institute of Chicago. She was recently in Spain organizing an exhibition about contemporary Spanish architecture and design.

2

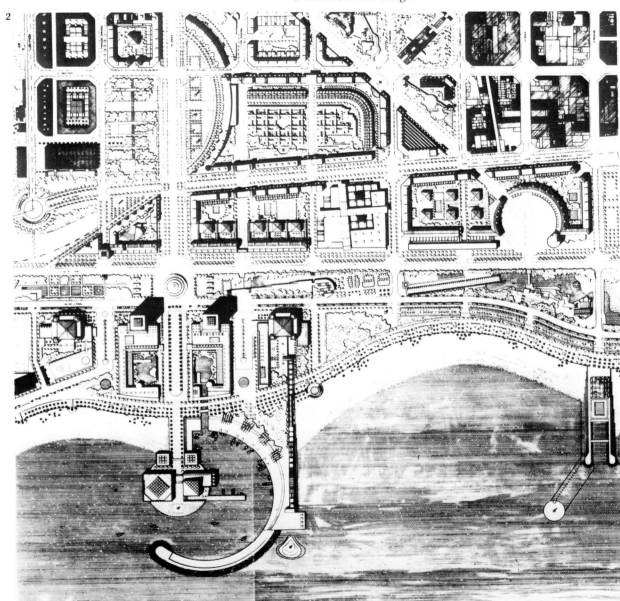

The Architect and the Classical Archaeologist

The architect is an essential part of any major archaeological excavation, particularly in classical Graeco-Roman sites throughout the Mediterranean region. Most sites are very rich with architectural remains of multiple periods, sometimes dating back several millennia. They are complex and difficult when they contain material of several cultural periods in close proximity to each other.

Archaeologists need architects for several reasons. First, they must work in close association with architects in order to have precise reference and location grids for their trenches, pits, cavities and channels. Second, they need the guidance of knowledgeable architects in identifying architectural remains. Finally, they depend upon the architects' expertise to piece together and restore, if only on paper, the remains of a given building from another era.

When beginning a new excavation location, the architect makes a careful survey with a theodolite and other surveying tools. The Cartesian grid is usually the standard method of locating horizontal points, and such a grid is extended into the new area from already established datum reference points and lines. The archaeologist's trenches are defined by these grid boundaries, and with the addition of precise elevation points, every find can be attributed to an exact location, both horizontally and vertically.

Architects working on Mediterranean sites must be familiar with standard components of classical architecture. The weathering of fragments may make identification difficult, but every piece found must be accounted for, if it has any discernible features. Although classical architecture generally follows a predictable pattern, variations from the norm occur frequently and must be understood for a correct restoration. Since ancient masons had the ability to cut marble blocks accurately to one millimeter, careful measurement of these blocks is required to insure an authentic reconstruction of a marble building.

Although photography is an indispensable tool for archaeology, it cannot replace the architect's measured drawings of extant remains. Photography does not discriminate between a random field stone and one used for a rubble wall foundation. The architect prepares an accurate drawing which locates all architectural evidence and suppresses or eliminates any irrelevant material. The archaeologist guides the architect in identifying the building foundations of different periods, particularly in a compressed situation where various architectural remains might be separated by mere centimeters. The archaeologist makes the decision as to which ruins are preserved and which are removed when it is impossible to simultaneously reveal all evidence. The responsible architect records every phase and level in detail, however, with measured plans, sections, and elevations.

It takes a minimum of at least ten years, from initial site excavation and documentation to final restored drawings for publication, to complete the story of a single building. The archaeologist prepares a complete text, with the architect's assistance, describing not only the physical characteristics of the remains but also the defense of the reconstruction based on actual evidence, comparative material, and historical context. A responsible publication includes measured drawings of individual blocks and identifiable fragments so that other scholars have the information available to agree with or dispute the given restoration. The architect's drawings provide not only accurate measurements, but they also exhibit any missing structural information based on engineering principles appropriate for the period.

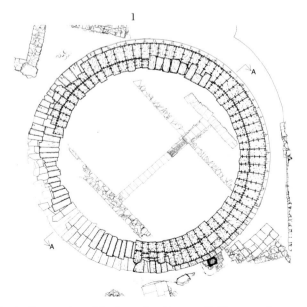

Fig. 1: Extant plan of the Rotunda of Arsinoe II. The entry door is located at the bottom of the plan.

The excavation, documentation, and reconstruction of the Rotunda of Arsinoe II, Sanctuary of the Great Gods, Samothrace, Greece (288-281 B.C.), largest closed round building known in Greek architecture, was begun by American excavators in 1938. Allowing time off for World War II, it took forty years to identify and measure the numerous remains, reconstruct the engineering of the missing roofs (the original Hellenistic roof was replaced by a completely different structural scheme during the reign of Augustus), and present the visualization of the building during its various phases.

An interesting problem to be solved was the configuration and design of the entry door. The Rotunda's circular marble walls rested on a base composed of a euthynteria course and three step courses. The extant euthynteria and step blocks had radial joints, and the remains of the foundation indicated that this base was consistent for the circumference of the building. One surviving wall block, however, had a finished surface of its joint end which wasn't the correct angle for a radial joint. Using trigonometric calculations, it was discovered that this angle was correct for an orthogonal cutting into the circular plan. The block was thus identified as a door block and proved that the entry was cut orthogonally into the wall rather than radially. Careful examination of the surviving foundation blocks revealed a subtle deviation of the placement of dowel holes for the missing euthynteria and step blocks as well as an enigmatic cutting in the foundation which was parallel to the radial joints of the building (fig. 1). This evidence not only located the door on the foundation, but it suggested orthogonal steps and threshold for the door (fig. 2). The break in the circular geometry of the base was taken up by low-rise parapet blocks which fit into the enigmatic cuttings, framing the entry steps and providing the necessary transition from radial to orthogonal steps (fig. 3).

John Kurtich

Mr. Kurtich is the Undergraduate Divisional Chair of the School of the Art Institute of Chicago and a Professor of Interior Architecture there as well. His restoration drawings of the Hellenistic and Roman versions of the Rotunda of Arsinoe II are being published by Princeton University Press, and he is currently writing a book on interior architecture with Garret Eakin which will be published by Van Nostrand Reinhold.

25

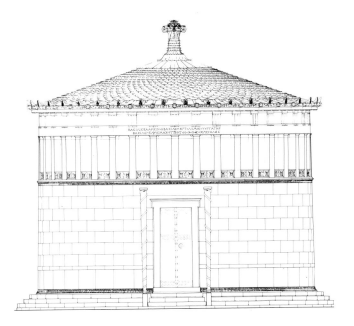

Fig. 2: Restored plan of the Rotunda of Arsinoe II. The upper half of the plan is at gallery level, and the lower half is at the orthostate level.

Fig. 3: Restored elevation of the Rotunda of Arsinoe II. The door is flanked by torches on parapet blocks.

On First Seeing Hagia Sophia

Approaching a masterpiece after a lifetime of expectation a fear arises. Perhaps after all the years of study and anticipation, the work will turn out to be a disappointment; perhaps one will fail to feel what has moved others so profoundly. With this in mind I went to Istanbul to see Hagia Sophia for the first time. Happily, once inside my fear fell away and the church surpassed all my expectations in a flood of climactic elation. Hours later, however, I was still asking questions about how it had all been done. In spite of years of homework before the trip, Hagia Sophia, built by Justinian in the sixth century, had much to teach me.

In the first place my expectations were not too high, they were not high enough. Even after seeing the Pantheon and St. Peter's in Rome, the Duomo in Florence, and St. Paul's in London, (three of them built centuries afterwards), Hagia Sophia raised my sights about what domed architecture could do, and then it fulfilled these new, higher expectations. This is what a masterpiece does, it expands your ideas about what is possible. In addition, Hagia Sophia's chief expressive vehicle, the scale of its light-filled enclosed space, works its magic on everyone. Masterpieces succeed universally.

Then the work of analysis began. Siegfried Kracauer's *Theory of Film* first taught me that an art form is most powerful when its unique aesthetic potential is its chief expressive vehicle. Only architecture can hold human beings and scale light-filled space to express meaning. The scale, the sheer containing bigness of Hagia Sophia, is the source of those first awe-struck moments. The great dome rises 56 meters above the floor, about the height of a fifteen-story building. Standing within it, one becomes a part of this brilliant, peaceful universe. An inspired device achieves this unified success, as my superb guidebook, *Strolling Through Istanbul* (now in revised form in the *Blue Guide to Istanbul*) by Hilary Sumner-Boyd and John Freely explained.

Magnificent as the dome is, it is the semidomes which are the key to the magic of Hagia Sophia. More important than expanding the nave to a basilica, they let us experience the full radiant height of the dome from any point in the interior — from the entrance in the front, the sides, directly beneath or from the galleries above. Without the semi-domes the effect of the dome would be diminished and become static. Anyone who studied the building, I thought, would be influenced by it, and

indeed most Turkish religious builders have been. The works of Sinan, the consummate architect of Suleyman the Magnificent, showed the continuing power of Hagia Sophia in his works a millenium later. What would have happened to the history of architecture if Brunelleschi, Michaelangelo or Sir Christopher Wren had traveled to Istanbul? Even though their domes may be larger or higher than Hagia Sophia's, you can only experience them from underneath, they form a part of the whole. The domes of Hagia Sophia are the whole, and one experiences them holistically.

But the experience also builds up to a climax. On our way to Istanbul we had walked the Sacred Way from the agora to the temples in Athens and Delphi. The advantages of such processionals could not have gone unnoticed by Hagia Sophia's builders, the architects Anthemius of Tralles and Isidorus of Miletus, both Greeks. They made the great tympani windows on the sides press in on the space to give it direction, to combine the longitudinal and the central plans, retaining the advantages of both. The semi-domes move forward, contained by the rectangle, while the larger dome floats freely above with the complete serenity of a circle. The combination of these domed spaces is more than the monumentality of the Pantheon plus the climactic upward and eastward movement of a church. The differences of east and west are transcended in a new form, more than the sum of its parts.

From the moment of entrance one sees this hosannah of arches and half domes to the rising crescendo of the great dome at once, resolving in a light-filled harmony where all restlessness fades away and peace lives. Indeed the dual theme of the church is proclaimed in the mosaic over the main entrance where Christ raises His right hand in blessing, and holds a book in His left with the inscription: "Peace be with you. I am the Light of the World." In the liturgy of the Eastern Church this theme is expressed in the climax of the service, which is not the elevation of the Host as in the western church, but the Kiss of Peace exchanged by the Emperor and the Patriarch in the center of the golden light of the dome.

No wonder that when Sultan Mehmet II entered Hagia Sophia on the 29th of May, 1453 he converted it immediately into a mosque, for its forms were eminently adaptable to the religion of Islam. In the seventeenth century Evliya Celebi wrote,

Sally A. Kitt Chappell

this mosque, which has no equal on earth, can only be compared to the tabernacle of the seventh heaven, and its dome to the cupola of the ninth. All of those who see it remain lost in contemplating its beauties; it is the place where heavenly inspiration descends into the minds of the devout and which gives a foretaste even here below of the Garden of Eden. Sultan Murat IV, who took great delight in this incomparable mosque, erected a wooden enclosure within it near the southern door, and when he went to prayer on Friday caused cages containing a great number of singing birds, and particularly nightingales, to be hung there, so that their sweet notes, mingled with those of the muezzins' voices, filled the mosque with a harmony approaching to that of paradise. Every night in the month of Ramadan, the two thousand lamps lighted there and the lanterns containing wax tapers perfumed with camphor pour forth streams of light upon light; and in the center of the dome a circle of lamps represents in letters as finely formed as those of Yakut Musta'sime, that text of the Kuran: 'God is the light of the heavens and of the earth.'

In the peace and light of its radiant spaces, faith and knowledge celebrate their divine union, wed in the sanctuary of Hagia Sophia, Holy Wisdom.

After a bi-coastal undergraduate education at Mills and Smith College, Chappell came to the University of Chicago for an M.A. and then went to Northwestern University for a Ph.D. in Art History where she wrote her dissertation on the Prairie School architect Barry Byrne. Currently she is Professor of Art History at DePaul University.

27

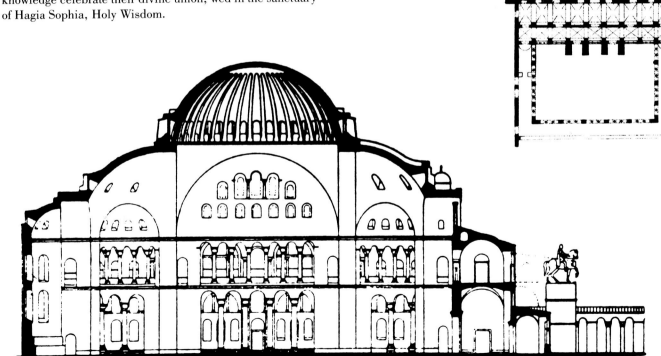

Fig. 1: Plan and section of Hagia Sophia, after Gurlitt and v.Sybel

A Note From Hiroshima

Hiroshima has had few buildings with powerful architectural associations, beyond the striking Torii gate in the sea at the Itsukushima Shrine in nearby Miyajima, and the damaged domed building left as a memorial to the first atomic bomb blast of August 6, 1945 . . . a dramatic ruin that was incorporated into the plan of the Peace Memorial Park and Museum by Kenzo Tange (1955). But Kisho Kurokawa recently designed a building that is an important example of its type and a fitting memorial to the city's cataclysmic past. The new (1988) Hiroshima City Museum of Contemporary Art sits overlooking the city, sunken somewhat into the mountain top to blend into the wooded landscape. Well designed and detailed right down to the furnishings, it has the architect's idea of "symbiosis" as its central notion. This is a philosophy in which he creates a new Japanese architecture, by using the best architectural elements and imagery from western and eastern sources.

The building accommodates temporary exhibitions and showings of the permanent collection in two different longitudinal wings that are joined at the center by a donut-like rotunda that at first evokes flying-saucers from science fiction. More to the point, it is a technologically conceived bomb crater, a domed entrance without the dome. The perfection of its circle is further broken by a conical turret at the entrance, and a slit in the circle that looks back at the city that has been rebuilt over the past half century. The paving that encircles the columns of this organizing rotunda incorporates stones discolored and damaged in the bomb blast. The approach stairway to the rotunda evokes the worlds before and after that fateful day by incorporating existing older stone steps adjacent to a new cut stone staircase. In addition to holding the traditional media of painting and sculpture, the museum showcases video in areas specially designed by the architect. To my knowledge, this is a "first" for an art museum.

Chicago Architectural Club members, the international art and architectural public; everyone should be made aware of this important building. It is well worth the trip, as much for instance as a journey to see James Stirling's Museum in Stuttgart or a Richard Meier's Museum in Frankfurt. It effectively deals with new technology and the arts, as well as providing a number of associations that remind one of this city's place in modern history.

John Zukowsky

John Zukowsky is Curator of Architecture at the Art Institute of Chicago. *He has written and edited a number of books such as* Hudson River Villas, Mies Reconsidered *and* Chicago Architecture: 1872-1922. *He was recently in Japan for the presentation of the Pritzker Prize to Frank Gehry at the Todai-ji Temple.*

Fig. 1: Exterior of the Rotunda
Fig. 2: Bird's Eye-View drawing by Kisho Kurokawa

1

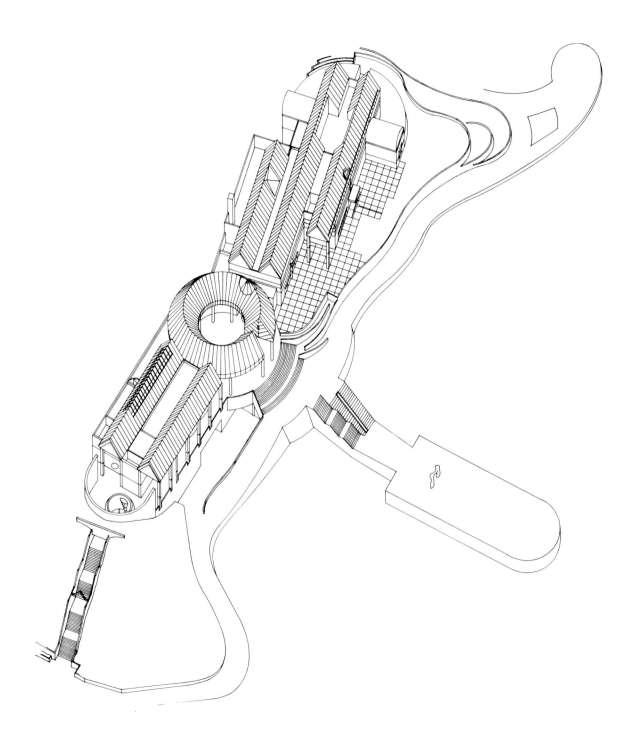

Ah Canada: Safdie's National Gallery

The new National Gallery of Canada in Ottawa by Moshe Safdie is a building of great strength and presence. Multiple and complex in its response to its programs — a museum, an urban set piece, a national symbol, it follows similar strategies in its use of materials and forms. The building has two major elements, a highly visible axial processional way, begun and finished in polygonal, crystalline spaces, and several layers of carefully rationalized, and generally neutral gallery spaces and the attendant, large areas needed to support them.

The gallery spaces are generally shaped to reinforce the character of the work exhibited, and several interior courts (one developed as a formal garden by Cornelia Oberlander, who also designed the sunken garden/amphitheater along the south flank of the building) serve to orient visitors in each of the several sections. The galleries are also elaborately served by natural light brought in through a system of long and mirrored light wells, controlled by the requisite computerized monitoring system.

The gallery occupies a site at the junction of the Rideau Canal and the Ottawa River called Nepean Point. Initially used for transhipment between the river traffic and the much smaller canal boats that descend an impressive series of locks just upstream on the Rideau, the site, and especially the great hall, is now used as a viewing platform to consider the surrounding scene. This sense of discovery is historically important, for Nepean Point memorializes the visits here in 1613 and 1615 of Samuel de Champlain, who claimed North America for France.

Standing in the great hall, the modern explorer encounters a vast panorama. Fanning out in a great southern arc, one sees Ottawa and the monuments of its history and development: the National Capitol Complex, with its polygonal parliamentary library, patterned after the chapter houses of English cathedrals, and in turn echoed by the crystalline figure of Safdie's pavilion; the sheer cliffs through which the Rideau Canal and its locks were cut; the Chateau Laurier, the city's great confection of a railroad hotel; the smaller buildings of the Lower Town district of earliest Ottawa; and the Notre Dame Basilica. These are the monuments of the success of European settlement in Canada — government, transportation, commerce, manufacture, propagation and maintenance of the faith, all seen to be successful and self-confident. To the north, obscured in part by the galleries, lies Hull, the French city

across the river in Quebec. Here, despite the recent heavy investment of public dollars, is a town and a region still rather colonial in aspect, self-image and its relentless depression caused by attitudes, habits and economic realities which are largely extractive and subtractive.

Along the diagonal, between a successful Ottawa and marginal Hull, is the Ottawa River which runs for nearly 500 miles to the northwest, dividing English speaking Ontario and French speaking Quebec. The vastness and emptiness of Canada (it is just about the same size as the United States with only about one tenth the population) has been a central subject in the history of the country as it has transformed itself from a conglomeration of French and English colonies, to a dominion of the British Empire, to an independent, multilingual nation.

It is the chief success of Safdie's building that instead of presenting to a visitor at the end of the long walk up the formal promenade of the National Gallery a great and representative work of art, he offers the greatness of the country. For it is the land itself which gives Canadians their opportunity to become a distinctive culture. Both French and British Canadians trace their cultural roots to a colonial past that was accepted as correct. As colonials, when that ordering power was removed, they felt adrift and without anchor. Now as they consider their future, this building helps them take a bold, inquisitive and reflective stance.

Two elements of the collections in the galleries suggest that this understanding of their Canadianness will come from introspection and observation about their natural and cultural heritage, not from some attitude derived from the heroic stance of the early explorers who saw the wilderness as a vastness to be gotten through or a treasure box to be looted. One is the work of the Group of Seven, a loose association of Canadian artists of the first half of this century who took the land as their subject. Those familiar with modern art can see in their work ideas, forms and techniques that appear to emerge from almost every strain of representational expression from Courbet to Hockney. Yet if one follows the axis that Safdie has offered in the great hall, it is clear that the particular form developed by these artists derives most powerfully from the distinctive content of the Canadian landscape. What seem initially abstractions of form, color and texture are more often in fact very sensitive responses to the actual images, textures and reflections that give the Canadian wilderness its unique character.

This ability to see the particular in what might seem at first a vast generality is also present in the work in the galleries devoted to the art of the Inuit, the native peoples of the arctic region. Today, Canadians of British and French heritage are a minority. The immigration from other countries of the British Commonwealth — Jamaica, Hong Kong, India, Nigeria, as well as from Europe, the Middle East and southeast Asia — means that the Canadian culture that emerges from this rich mix will be new and undominated by those who might claim the precedence of earlier settlement. This further means that the view of Canada of those who are most marginal — the native peoples, who have largely attempted to maintain their own traditions — may have much to teach their fellow citizens. Particularly impressive are the Inuit drawings of groups of things, usually animals. Here is a kind of expression in which a given stencil-like order is established and then within that order the individuality and differentness of each are slowly revealed as one studies the image comparatively, until, whether the group is of geese or seals or children, one begins to note that within the similarities, the artist clearly sees those elements that distinctively give each individual their own personality, character and presence. This is a combinatory skill, where the forest and the trees are each seen for their own special qualities without losing either the nature of the whole or the uniqueness of the individual.

This opportunity for observation, reflection and contemplation that Safdie offers in his panorama as it sums up what it might be to be Canadian, is the greatest success of the building. If one begins to consider the building alone, its defects, more than its virtues begin to attract attention. As anyone familiar with his first famous commission, Habitat, knows, an extremely strong idea was compromised by the weakness of many details. This is again the case in the National Gallery. Whether one considers the juxtaposition of the structural concrete and the Tadoussac granite of the entry and promenade, the sense of orientation to and within the galleries, or the manner in which individual galleries are developed, the initial appearance that the building has been conceived as a system is undermined by the failure to follow the implications of that system to meaningful resolution.

As for the materials, this means that the concrete, which is the structure, seems too light, spindly and on occasion unable to do the work intended, while the granite reads as wallpaper, not the great, strong lithic elements one might imagine. Regarding orientation, the plans and sections make clear his interest in modernist patterning, but neglects that visitors are not likely trained in the conventions of that system, and thus find themselves reduced to following the arrows on signs placed in the halls to find one's way around. There is no sense of marche, or any other consequent procession or progression in the museum, once one has left the great hall. The building and its galleries feel far more like the additive, accretive galleries of the Metropolitan in New York than Pope's ordered and understandable National Gallery in Washington or the Shepley Rutan & Coolidge block of the Art Institute of Chicago. In the galleries themselves, the handling of details where wall and ceiling vault intersect, or corners are turned, or doors are opened in the wall, or partition walls divide a space to accommodate the art on display, all serve to remind one of Safdie's disinterest in this kind of problem.

However, these flaws are not so severe as to make the design unsuccessful on the whole. The panorama that is offered as one enters the gallery, and before one finds the collection serve to give the visitor the opportunity to consider the entire idea of a National Gallery, particularly in a Nation whose heritage has so many sources.

Kevin Harrington

Kevin Harrington teaches architectural history at the Illinois Institute of Technology. He has a bachelor of arts from Colgate University and a doctorate from Cornell University. An editor and contributor to Mies van der Rohe: Architect as Educator, *he has also published on Ludwig Hilberseimer. He is completing a monograph on Mies's design of the IIT Campus.*

Ida Noyes Hall at the University of Chicago:
A Building to Engender Students:

The metaphor of the body challenges architecture to reconsider its classically-grounded tradition of anthropomorphism and come to terms with the debate over what is cultural as opposed to natural, or gendered as opposed to sexual, and how those distinctions are constructed and used. These questions have been critical to architecture ever since classicism was placed into question during the Romantic period. One building which embodies these issues as they were debated around World War I is Ida Noyes Hall at the University of Chicago, built between 1913-1916 as the social center for female students, who were explicitly intended to recover their genders through the use of the building.

Ida Noyes Hall stands at the intersection of two discourses. One is about the architectural tradition in which gender expresses the purpose of a given building. The other is about the purposes of higher education for women, which at the time of its construction involved two parties who were disputing the nature/nurture debate: eugenicists vs. euthenists. Eugenicists feared that college education was diverting WASP women from reproducing. Euthenists sought a significant reform of housekeeping, the feminine domain of the family, and ultimately the public domain of the neighborhood, city, and nation. Marion Talbot, Dean of Women at the University of Chicago, professor of sociology, and the initiator of its Department of Household Administration, was a leading euthenist. Head of an advisory committee of University women, Talbot worked with the Trustees and the architect, Charles Coolidge of Shepley, Rutan, and Coolidge, and played a critical role in planning Ida Noyes Hall as a settlement house for university women, analogous to Chicago's Hull House.

Unlike Coolidge's earlier buildings for male students, Hutchinson Commons, Reynold's Club, Mitchell Tower, and Bartlett Gymnasium, Ida Noyes Hall did more than confirm its users' gender. As Talbot's mentor John Dewey aimed to "reconstruct" his students at the University of Chicago's Laboratory School of 1903, Ida Noyes Hall would "reconstruct" the feminine characteristics lacking in its users. Professor Sophonisba Breckinridge explained at the inauguration,

> Women have lacked facilities for the cultivation of certain social arts and . . . have had no equipment . . . [to] develop in themselves, in each other and in the men students those expressions of a gay spirit which both beautify life and add to the collective powers of the group . . . Ida Noyes . . . will add greatly to the efficiency . . . and commercial value of the training given in classroom and laboratory . . . After a little

while, it will be impossible for a student to lose a position for which she is professionally well prepared because her . . . general bearing [is] constrained and awkward.

Breckinridge affirmed the value of the traditional female role for society and professional women, and indicated its absence in her own constituency. Most of the university's 1200 female students came from modest backgrounds, to train for a gainful career, usually teaching school. Despite an infamously low marriage rate for college-educated women, Talbot and Breckinridge assumed that their students would eventually leave their jobs to raise families. Their book of 1912, *The Modern Household*, saw the moderate-income student becoming a new type of housewife adapted to the emerging consumer economy. She would spend the family's income efficiently, demand quality in products no longer made at home, and save money to form the leisure activities and tastes of the family. Influenced by Chicago's Arts and Crafts movement and Jane Addams' settlement house movement for low-income immigrant women, Talbot provided an alternative model to the conspicuous consumption of the very wealthy. Management, science, art, and "natural" grace were fundamentally intertwined in this notion of the educated woman as the guardian of the consumer and leisure economy.

All parties agreed that Ida Noyes Hall should be "homelike," as much of women's college architecture had been. The particular architectural form that reform should take was less evident. Talbot's program did not differ greatly from the men's center, including a gym, a refectory, a sunporch for meals, and a clubhouse with a theater, but she argued that these functions should be compressed into a single unit exemplifying the values of economy and efficiency. Her point was that the integrative social function performed by women should be reinforced by an architectural integration of multiple purposes in a domestic form. Coolidge gave the building a T-shaped form with one end hooked to enframe a cloistered garden. Its three wings intersect in a spacious lobby designed as a "living hall" with a large, open staircase and wide openings to the adjacent rooms — the emblem of the hospitable domesticity developed Style summer cottages.

Talbot recognized that much of the building's architectural character would depend on the site and its relationship to the compact quadrangles of the campus, tangential to the long Midway Plaisance:

> I hope it is not a vain dream to imagine [Ida Noyes] clothed in an architectural garb which will not only be more convenient

but more expressive of the 20th century woman in Chicago, USA than is the medieval, monastic and dungeonlike type of some of the other buildings! I would be more than glad to sacrifice its location on the Midway . . . to secure a spirit of freedom, lightness and aspiration which might not harmonize with the buildings already planned for the Midway.

She was familiar with the alternatives presented by the classical Woman's Building of the 1893 Exposition and Wright's Robie House of 1909, then within view of the Ida Noyes site. The classical orders had been indelibly gender-typed in antiquity, and gender informed Wright's translations of body images into landscape images in his Prairie houses. Talbot had played a part in the Woman's Building, which, it was said, epitomized feminine grace through its Ionic and Corinthian loggias. Women's college architecture had not produced a new type explicitly associated with femininity. Given monumental frontage along the Midway, Talbot accepted an adaptation of the University's medieval idiom. But she and her colleagues were adamant that young women, as consumers, be made aware of the connotations of architecture and interior decoration. How was the collegiate medieval, with its mural expanses, to achieve an effect of grace?

Ruskin guided Coolidge and those who later interpreted the building under professor Edith Flint, who helped plan Ida Noyes. The foliage of the maidenly Corinthian order was loosed from its classicism to become the "naturalistic" vine of *The Stones of Venice*, and the leitmotif of Ida Noyes. It climbs the banister of the stair and transforms the beams of the main rooms into ripe arbors. Its touch is the caress of mother nature, which civilizes and embellishes the masculine product of the building. For Ruskin, medieval architecture encompassed both genders in a manner superior to classical architecture:

> See if it looks as if it had been built by strong men; if it has the sort of roughness, and largeness, and nonchalance, mixed in places with the exquisite tenderness which seems always to be the sign-manual of the broad vision, and massy power of men who can see past the work they are doing.

"Tenderness" was supplied by the "tendril" of the vine in tracery and ornament — "a softer element . . . peculiar to the Gothic," which was "indicative both of higher civilization and gentler temperament." If female nature could instruct men to see beyond their force, in Ida Noyes women would be taught to identify with nature, in order to fulfill that service.

Comparing Coolidge's Hutchinson Commons with his Ida Noyes refectory demonstrates this. Dining was the critical test for gender in the consumer society. Lofty, Hutchinson Commons claimed the tradition of Christ Church, Oxford. Its men would fulfill a prestigious history under portraits of University role-models. But Ida Noyes's has two walls of enormous windows bringing sunlight to the garden of ornament within, culminating in a vine-covered ceiling. Nature would inspire, instead of history.

Students practiced this lesson in the third-floor Tudor sunporch overlooking the Midway. With sunlight streaming through the terrace doors, this Tudor room proclaimed the euthenic cult of household hygiene. Here women entertained friends with meals they had prepared in an up-to-date kitchenette, served on handmade Arts and Crafts plates and mugs, meant to foster individualism, naturalism and gaiety in an industrial urban context. The furnishings were selected by University women from diverse places and periods to reconstruct the cumulative character of a country house, teaching the pluralist values of eclecticism. Truth to nature was the common value.

For the building's inauguration on the University's 25th anniversary, Talbot commissioned a masque by her former student Lucine Finch. Its scenes are recorded in Jessie Botke's murals in the theater. The didactic idea of the building was the subject, and the cycle begins when a young woman crowned with flowers and identified with nature, presents herself to Alma Mater. In sequence she earns the University's gifts: physical robustness, a husband, and knowledge. The cycle closes when the City arrives to claim her skills. Education is no end in itself; its justification is social service. The lesson identifies women with nature, and nature with service.

The reconstruction of women as nature paralleled the reconstruction of nature as a park in the therapeutic garden city. Women and nature could restore the troubled industrial city, but both required cultivation to achieve that. Dewey's and Talbot's process is like that advocated by Ruskin to create a "naturalistic vine:" neither a "sensualist" untrammeled vine, nor a "purist" vine in servitude, but rather one which serves with gaiety.

Katherine Fischer Taylor

Katherine Taylor teaches architectural history at the University of Chicago. Recently completing her PhD at Harvard University, she is continuing her study of 19th century urbanism.

33

On Spiro Kostof's *A History of Architecture: Settings and Rituals*

From the moment that it appeared in 1985, most critics have agreed that Spiro Kostof's *A History of Architecture* is a landmark achievement. In their view, Kostof succeeded by taking a familiar genre and infusing it with new life. The most comprehensive world survey in English since Bannister Fletcher's *History of Architecture on the Comparative Method*, Kostof's book combines vivid, often brilliantly written descriptions with sound analysis based on the work of specialists in the various periods. This is not a negative judgment, but it greatly underestimates Kostof's achievement.

To understand how effectively Kostof subverted some of the basic assumptions that lie behind the architectural history survey, it is important to reconsider for a moment the survey as we know it. Obsession with history was part of the prodigious program of Western thought. Spawned by the Enlightenment, the program gained urgency with the advent of the Industrial Revolution, and it brought a kind of order to the world by the systematic collection of knowledge. Modern man had as his goal not just understanding, but control. He was searching for the tools which could determine the rules for human activity.

A similar strategy guided most writers of architectural history between the 18th and early 20th century, from Fischer von Erlach to Frankl in the German speaking world, from Félibien to Choisy in France, and from Fergusson or Bannister Fletcher in England. They would chart the rise and fall of the great styles of architecture in order to demonstrate, explicitly or implicitly, the basic principles that seemed to govern the most successful monuments of each great period. It was not a problem if the procession of monuments from the pyramids to Versailles also happened to coincide almost exactly with the most conspicuous buildings created by each era's most powerful people. The West's religious and political traditions had long sanctified this union between power and beauty. Whether the writer was a proponent of classical styles or the Gothic, the belief that beauty obeyed certain fixed rules was rarely questioned. The task was to decide what those rules of beauty were.

Most 19th and early 20th century historians preferred a cyclical or dialectic plot. In the one, a great style might grow from a vigorous archaic beginning through full bodied maturity to an over-ripe but often brilliant final phase. Alternatively, one style might follow another, with artists reacting to the work of

the previous era by inverting key formal characteristics, creating a pendulum-like action.

While the advent of 20th century European modernism did surprisingly little to alter previous assumptions or organizational schemes, it did graft onto them an entirely new set of attitudes and a new chapter. When treating architecture since 1750, European modernists such as Pevsner or Giedion invented a new strategy. Their story of modern architecture, far from cyclical, was based on a single straight line of development from historical styles to the new, universal modernist style. Most of these writers believed, as did the classicists, that there were standards of absolute beauty. But when it came to the architecture of their time, they also relied on moral imperatives extrinsic to architecture. Firmness and commodity became extremely important, even determining factors in producing delight.

Kostof clearly knows the modernist tradition in architectural history. He has written with understanding about the works of Sigfried Giedion, the most prodigious and powerful of all modernist architectural historians. In his Preface, Kostof tells us with characteristic brevity and clarity some of the ways his history departs from Giedion and modernist historians. For Kostof the history of architecture is not just the chronicle of the great architects and canonical buildings of the Western tradition. It includes structures of all types, from non-Western as well as Western lands, from the most humble to the most pretentious. "Haghia Sophia and Versailles are here," Kostof tells us, "but so are igloos and 19th century malt-kilns; the ducal palaces of Urbino and Mantua are discussed within the larger frame of the city-form; the Romans share their chapter with the 'barbarian adversaries,' the Dacians, and the tribes of the sub-Sahara."

This passage also makes clear another way in which Kostof's history departs from most previous architectural surveys. He is not primarily interested in style or single heroic creators of art. Although he does discuss the style of buildings and major architects, his aim is "the story of humans taking possession of the land and shaping communities through the act of building." He focuses on architecture not so much as a fine art, but as a social act that takes place in the city or the larger landscape.

Taken separately, none of these propositions seems particularly surprising today, and the extent of Kostof's break with traditional approaches is not readily apparent. Though Kostof often discusses the typical, rather than the extraordinary, the major monuments are there, and so are the familiar plot devices. Histories of urbanism have covered subjects discussed by Kostof, and there are studies of the vernacular landscape. In its general configuration and organization, the book appears to be similar to many other histories, from the earliest examples, to Trachtenberg and Hyman's recent *Architecture from Pre-History to Post-Modernism*.

Kostof admits as much in his Preface, which reads: "This book is something of a compromise. It is a general survey of architectural history that tries to reconcile the traditional grand canon of monuments with a broader, more embracing view of the built environment." He kept the general format of the architectural history in part because it was a necessity. His topics are the ones on which research has been done. For other subjects he might have wished to discuss there was simply no available research. It is also likely that Kostof wanted his book to have a familiar feel. His unassuming manner, and his refusal to suggest that errors by previous authors required him to set matters straight, allows the reader to start reading his work like the entertaining and partially familiar story which it is. Only part-way through the book is it apparent how radically he has departed from the viewpoints of Fletcher or Giedion.

Other surveys have included non-Western traditions, but only when they can be sequestered. Whenever possible Kostof mixes Western buildings with those of different traditions, in order to undercut the Eurocentric and ethnocentric assumptions that underlie the traditional history of architecture. He uses traditional plot devices, including dialectic and cyclical developments within a given tradition, but the story is multi-directional and more fragmentary than usual, with numerous juxtapositions of time, scale, and place. Man as the heroic god-like creator of modernist Western thought is not at the center of this book.

Wherever he is found, in Kostof's book man is a social creature who is obliged to share the world with plants, animals and with the land itself. This abiding interest in the character and history of the land is one of the most basic features of the book. Shunning the traditional threads of stylistic or structural progression, Kostof finds other connections to demonstrate the variety of ways landscapes were created by individuals and societies.

The book's greatest departure from tradition lies in its most basic assumptions. Kostof is a native of Turkey, a land poised precariously between East and West, and he lives in an adopted land as an academic. Perhaps these conditions help to detach him from the absolute standards of the classicists and the moral, social and political imperatives of the 20th century avant garde. Although he is willing to judge how well a structure has fulfilled a society's purposes, he is rarely willing to judge the society. He is less interested in eternal verities than the shifting agreements man enters into in order to inhabit the planet.

This is a book that speaks to and reflects our time as powerfully as Giedion's did his. Giedion's book was a brilliant polemic for a generation which thought it had the answers, but this is a more accommodating manifesto. Kostof has no formula for remaking the world. He is more interested in trying to understand than coming to final judgment. His most important lesson is about the value of careful scrutiny of the entire world around us, and about the worth and dignity of human beings and their built creations wherever they are found.

Robert Bruegmann

Robert Bruegmann teaches architectural history at the University of Illinois at Chicago. He has a bachelors degree from Principia College and his doctorate from the University of Pennsylvania. He has taught and lectured widely, and this year is a fellow at the Buell Center at Columbia University. His multivolume work on Holabird & Roche / Holabird & Root will be published soon.

The Burnham Prize Competition

Burnham Prize Winner:
Jerry Johnson

Alternate:
Julie Gross

Honorable Mentions:
John MacManus
Deborah Moore (not illustrated)

Jury:
Harry Weese, representing the
American Academy in Rome

Terry Harkness, Professor of
Landscape Architecture at the
University of Illinois at Urbana

Sidney Robinson, Associate
Professor of Architecture at the
University of Illinois at Chicago

Gilbert Gorski, previous
Burnham Prize Winner

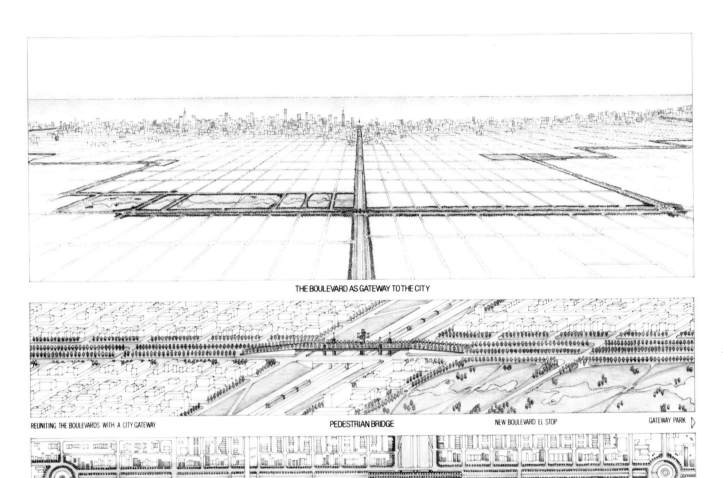

THE BOULEVARD AS GATEWAY TO THE CITY

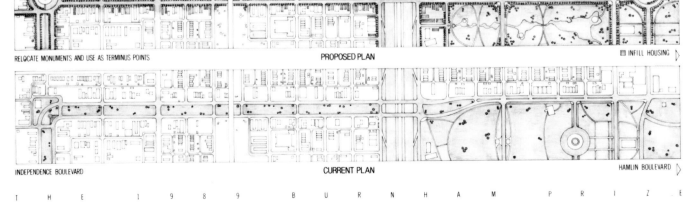

REUNITING THE BOULEVARDS WITH A CITY GATEWAY   PEDESTRIAN BRIDGE   NEW BOULEVARD EL STOP   GATEWAY PARK ▷

RELOCATE MONUMENTS AND USE AS TERMINUS POINTS   PROPOSED PLAN   ⊞ INFILL HOUSING ▷

INDEPENDENCE BOULEVARD   CURRENT PLAN   HAMLIN BOULEVARD ▷

THE 1989 BURNHAM PRIZE

38

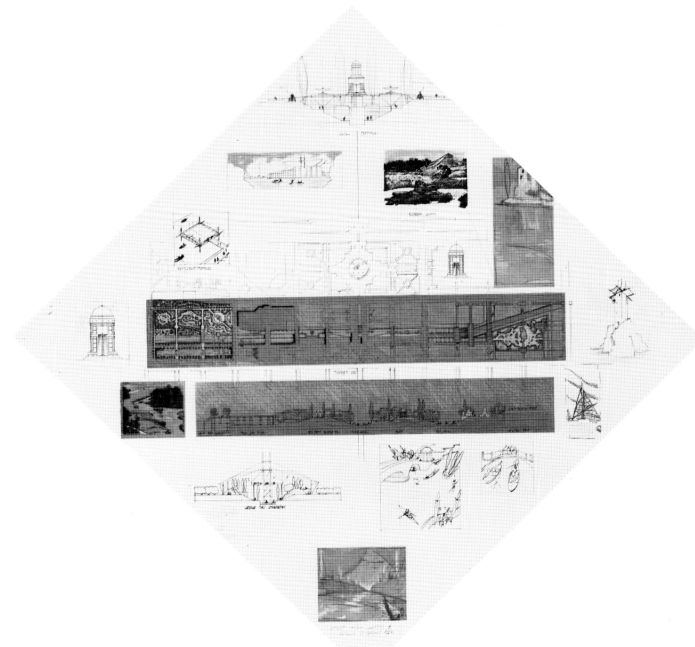

Chicago Architectural Club Members

Armbrust, Alan J.
Bauhs, William
Beckley, Robert M.
Beeby, Kirsten
Beeby, Thomas H.
Bonner Jr., Darcy R.
Booth, Laurence
Bowman, John
Bruegmann, Robert
Castillo, Phillip
Chapell, Sally A. Kitt
Clark, John W.
Clawson, Kim
Cohen, Stuart
Danker, Dirk W.
De Wit, Wim
Decker, Howard
Dieckmann, Laurence E.
Donchik, Vladimir G.
Doordan, Dennis P.
Doyle, Deborah
Drake, William
Eakin, Garret
Ellis, Peter G.
Fernandez, Ricardo J.
Florian, Paul
Frankel, Neil P.
Frisbee, Peter E.
Fugman, Robert
Gelick, Michael
Goettsch, James
Goldsmith, Myron
Gonzalez, Joseph A.
Gorski, Gilbert
Graham, Bruce J.
Greenspan, David
Gusevich, Miriam
Hacker, Julie
Hansen, David A.

Harrington, Kevin
Hasbrouck, Wilbert R.
Haymes, David A.
Hinds, George A
Horn, Gerald
Jahn, Helmut
Johnson, Karen
Johnson, Ralph
Kelley, Jack
Kemp, Kevin
Ketcham, William F.
Krause, Linda R.
Krueck, Ronald A.
Kurtich, John
Lahey, John C.
Landahl, Gregory W.
Landon, Peter
Langdon, Tannys
Law, James
Legge, Diane
Lohan, Dirk
Lustig, Michael
Madeyski, Wojciech
Manny Jr., Carter H.
McBride, William Alan
McCurry, Margaret
Metter, Andrew
Nagle, James L.
Naughton, Jack
Nelson, Linda Lee
Nereim, Anders
Nicholson, Ben
Novickas, Al
Olsen, Keith
Pappageorge, George C.
Phillips, Frederick
Potokar, Richard
Quinn, Kathryn
Rajkovich, Thomas Norman

Robinson, Sidney
Rogatz, Janet
Rudolph, Christopher H.
Saliga, Pauline
Schildknecht, Rainer
Schipporeit, George
Schneider-Criezis, Susan
Schroeder, Kenneth A.
Searl, Linda
Skvarla, Melvyn A.
Smith, Adrian D.
Solfisburg, Roy J.
Solomon, Richard Jay
Steevensz, Rene
Steinbrecher, Paul A.
Swan, David
Syvertson, John
Taylor, Katherine F.
Temple, Ann
Thompson, Patrick
Tigerman, Stanley
Ullman, Marvin
Valerio, Joseph M.
Van Zanten, David
Ventsch, Leslie
Weese, Ben
Weese, Cynthia
Welch, Thomas R.
Wheeler, Daniel Harding
Whitaker, Richard R.
White, Hub
Whiteman, John
Wierzbowski, Stephen
Wilson, Frederick
Wolf, Martin F.
Woodhouse, David
Yas, Stephen
Zukowsky, John

Works by Members of the
Chicago Architectural Club

Gilbert Gorski

Gilbert Gorski graduated with a bachelor of architecture degree from the Illinois Institute of Technology in 1978. Until 1988 he was an Associate Principal with Lohan Associates where he was the project designer for a number of buildings, including the World Headquarters for the McDonald's Corporation and the Oceanarium expansion to the Shedd Aquarium. Mr. Gorski was awarded the Chicago Architectural Club's 1987 Burnham Prize for study at the American Academy in Rome. He presently has his own practice concentrating on architectural drawings and paintings.

Forum of Trajan
Rome

While in Rome I completed a drawing of Trajan's Forum as it appeared in the second century, in collaboration with Professor James Packer of Northwestern University and Kevin Sarring of Harry Weese & Associates, who have been jointly studying the forum since 1972. Upon returning to the United States, Professor Packer commissioned three more images, funded by grants from the Samuel H. Kress Foundation of New York and the Graham Foundation of Chicago, for a monograph on Trajan's Forum.

42

43

George A. Hinds

Venetian Sketchbook

Principal at HSW, Ltd., & Lenders' Architectural construction consulting firm, Mr. Hinds received a bachelor of architecture degree in 1949 and a master of city planning degree in 1953 from Yale University. He has worked with Smith, Hegner, and Moore in Colorado; Ralph Erskine in Sweden; the Philadelphia City Planning Commission and the Philadelphia Redevelopment Authority, where he was Acting Director of Planning. He has been an associate professor at ITB, Indonesia; the University of Kentucky, and Harvard University. He is a professor emeritus of the University of Illinois at Chicago, and a Fellow of the American Academy in Rome, having won the Rome Prize in 1983.

His work has received a Progressive Architecture *Design Award, a Distinguished Building Award and a Distinguished Interior Architecture Award from the Chicago Chapter of the AIA, and a Great Cities Project Design Award from the Ford Foundation. He has written articles for the* AIA Journal, Inland Architect, *and* Process International.

Being a reactive architect, I need stimulus and *ricordando* for a satisfactory balance in my existence. I always welcome the opportunity to rebuild in my mind the forms, details, proportion and scale of the masterpieces of the past, and so I sketch. Doing this outside of the dictates of the era that produced these masterpieces is an advantage which a student of the evolutionary process of design has over a student who is caught up in the stylistic forces that shape the architectural fashion of the day.

Stimulus is needed for growth and change, and reading and sketching can provide this stimulus. The process of rebuilding the architectural masterpieces can tolerate the intrusion of reactive thought and other stimuli that keep the language of architecture off-balance and vital. As Tafuri points out, too strict an adherence to the rules and vocabulary of a linguistic style, in this case the language of architecture, may result in the atrophy and eventual death of the style itself. These sketches were done as part of the graduate program in Italy that I direct for the University of Illinois at Chicago.

44

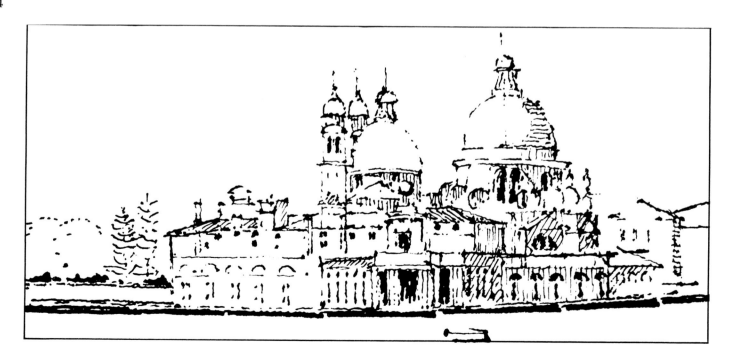

Sketches of Venice by George Hinds

Linda Krause

One of the good things about a grab-bag category is that one feels little compulsion to tie it all together in a nice, neat package. In fact, it's time to worry when the same style, theory, or program crops up in everything from offices to oratories. Happily, the designs in this group offer no such homogeneity. Similarly, my comments are fairly diffuse because different designs suggested different issues. If there is a loose thread that unites my essay it might be how architecture both responds to and creates a context.

A few years ago I witnessed what I thought was an anomaly when the modest modernist Quaker Company Building rose amid the "deco"-rated towers lining the Chicago River. Quaker seemed a throw-back to the post-war architectural idiom of Gordon Bunshaft. Utterly predictable, even formulaic, the building appeared to represent everything post-modernists decried. But if to some this was the very image of retrograde universal form, to others it might be an alternative to meretricious (and equally formulaic) essays in neo-moderne. Given this city's Miesian context, perhaps it was the post-modern buildings that were anomalous. One thing is certain, whether through survival or revival, modernism is alive and well in Chicago.

Nowhere is this clearer than in the entries of Peter Frisbee and Andy Metter. Both Frisbee's Northwestern Studio Building and Metter's Health Sciences Building pay homage to the modernist doctrine of functionalism. Frisbee's unpretentious work presents almost all the modernist markers (alas no roof garden) in a straightforward and unapologetic manner. Metter's building seems to take its cue from that child of modernism, English Brutalism. Like Stirling's work at Leicester and Cambridge, this university facility consists of clearly articulated, prismatic elements housing diverse functions.

While Frisbee and Metter preserve modernist ideals, Ron Krueck and Paul Florian deconstruct them. Their respective entries to the American Memorial Library competition assume a critical stance towards modernism's naturalized truths. How fitting that this challenge should take place in modernism's ideological birthplace.

The existing Amerika-Gedenkbibliothek, distant and banal descendant of Mies and Hilberseimer, is retained in both schemes. In his library addition, Krueck overlays, slices, dislocates and severs the now canonic grid. The rigid

orthogonals of the rear facade press against the central glazed space and create a tension, rather than resolution, between surface and volume. Paul Florian's additions are altogether lighter, freer, and more diverse. To the sober and spiritless original, Florian adds intriguing elements that turn the ensemble into a series of surprises and possibilities. Linking the various parts is a high wall — something of a minimalist Valhalla — inscribed with the names of German and American literary worthies. Thus, one may literally "read" the wall. But the wall may also be "read" metaphorically as barrier transformed into conduit. It suggests that walls may simultaneously impede and open. So Florian's wall reminds us that in Berlin (and elsewhere) walls intended to obstruct the flow of ideas, become the locus of free speech.

At Bard College, James Goettsch was also faced with designing a library addition. Explicitly modern, the addition nonetheless harmonizes with the 19th century building. Indeed, what Goettsch demonstrates is the shared origin of the late Greek Revival and modernism in earlier neo-Classicism. The great Pantheon-like rotunda recalls Jefferson's famous library at the University of Virginia with its attendant temples. For Jefferson the classical style and pure geometric forms suggested enlightenment. Goettsch makes enlightenment literal with a glass enclosed study.

Jefferson is also recalled in the new Chapel for Maryville Academy designed by Leslie Ventsch. Or perhaps it would be more accurate to say Palladio, by way of Jefferson. A covered walkway that connects the chapel and priests' residence, focuses and delimits the campus perspective. Ventsch composes the chapel facade with a Palladian motif of superimposed triangular roof elements.

In contrast to the academicism of Maryville, Linda Nelson's Hopewell Center seems simple and unprepossessing. Yet the composition of the campus presents a carefully constructed community for its handicapped clients. Here the campus center is not a processional route or an empty green space, but an archetypal shelter. The shelter, with its simultaneous suggestions of protection and isolation, appropriately serves as the halfway house between cloistered campus and outside world.

Though many of the preceding designs were additions, each of the architects chose to deviate either radically or subtly from the existing context. Despite its careful formalism, for instance, one would not mistake Ventsch's chapel for a Palladian or even neo-Palladian building. Opposing this tendency are the entries of Alan Armbrust and Kevin Kemp, where distinctions between old and new are intentionally blurred.

Armbrust's carefully detailed and nicely scaled addition to the Roosevelt School repeats the materials and style of the original building. Kemp's Northbrook Village Hall, though freestanding, was meant to replicate the English medieval revival style found in other Village buildings. Kemp's two illustrations show different stages in the design process. An early solution appears in the elevation drawing. The perspective view shows the facade as built. The earlier version was, to my thinking, the better composition. The taller tower, more emphatic entrance, and window wall gave the building a presence and variety lacking in the built version. Unfortunately, programmatic changes and local building codes diminished the most appealing aspects of this style.

The price one pays for the kind of stylistic homogeneity found in the school addition and village hall is anonymity. Success is measured in the degree of self-effacement willingly accepted by the designers. Armbrust and Kemp justified their designs as responsive to a specific local context. Yet I detect no Ruskinian zeal for medieval architecture or ornamental brickwork and I sense that different contexts would yield different styles.

This does not seem to be the case with Tom Rajkovich, whose persistent enthusiasm for Baroque and neo-Classical architecture has been well documented in these pages. His entry to the Korean Veterans' War Memorial competition, with its explicit references to 18th century funerary architecture, certainly affirms his continued interest in Romantic classicism.

Compared to the puerile and inane winning design, a platoon of larger-than-life soldiers traipsing through a formal arbor — that looks for all the world like an assault force of tree surgeons, Rajkovich's design is a model of sublime decorum. The pyramid and obelisks, time honored symbols of heroic self-sacrifice, are used to memorialize the Korean War dead. Yet do they? Is Romantic classicism an appropriate vehicle for remembering soldiers lost in that conflict? Unlike the Vietnam War Veterans' memorial, this design does not ask us to rethink the nature of memorials and, by extension, what is being memorialized. Rather, Rajkovich's design presents us with a familiar (and therefore unquestioned) set of symbols that perpetuate the Romantic style and the Romantic mythification of war.

Bruce Graham's Ludgate project brings to mind another war, WWII. Over now subterranean railway tracks, Graham places three office buildings. Their exposed steel frames have a rather spectral appearance, recalling the pathetic skeletal remains of blitzed London. (And Ludgate was an area especially hard hit.) But the revealed skeletons also suggest Britain's significant role in the development of modern structural iron and steel. Fittingly, the buildings are placed on a site formerly occupied by a 19th century railway station. Marvels of structural engineering, such buildings spawned the technology that made possible Graham's new construction.

Cultural, Institutional, and Urban Design Projects

Alan J. Armbrust

The 5000 sq. ft. school addition creates four kindergarden classrooms with amenities scaled to the children. The formal entry separates the children from the older students, providing an independent identity, and creating a "school within a school." Brick and synthetic terra-cotta with ceramic tile insets were chosen to harmonize with the existing 1930's structure, and scaled down to address its function.

A project architect with O'Donnell Wicklund Pigozzi and Peterson, he received a bachelor of architecture from the Illinois Institute of Technology in 1980. He attended the American Academy in Rome as the 1988 Chicago Architectural Club's Burnham Prize fellow, and received honorable mention in the Chicago Tribune's competition to design an alternative to the 1992 world's fair. His work has been exhibited at the Art Institute of Chicago, the Frumkin Struve Gallery and the Chicago Public Library Cultural Center.

Roosevelt School, Park Ridge District #64
Park Ridge, Illinois

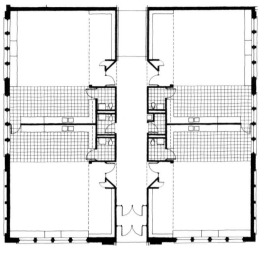

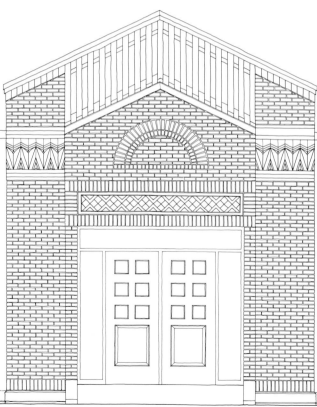

Firm: O'Donnell Wicklund Pigozzi and Peterson
Staff: Alan Armbrust assisting Ray Pigozzi
Photography: Howard N. Kaplan

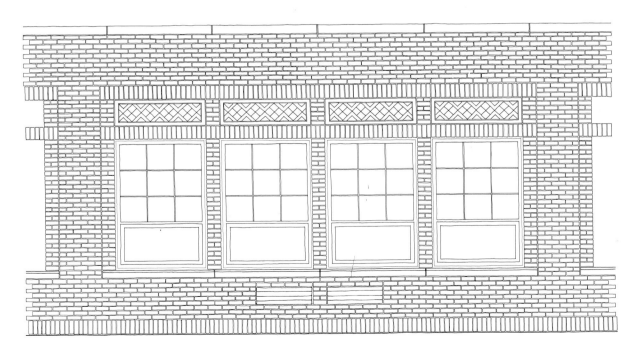

John W. Clark

A partner in Cordogan, Clark & Associates, John Clark received his degree from the University of Illinois in 1977, with graduate study in urban planning. Previously he worked with Hammond Beeby and Babka, and Gelick Foran Associates. He has taught at the School of the Art Institute of Chicago, and has been a visiting design juror at the University of Illinois and Illinois Institute of Technology. His work has been included in numerous exhibitions and is in the collection of the Art Institute of Chicago.

Performing Arts Center
Towson, Maryland

The Performing Arts Center accommodates the teaching of theater arts and music, as well as serving as a performance center for the university and its surrounding community.

Positioned on the crest of a wooded slope, the facility has the form of an academic village: a group of independently articulated theaters and pavilions which is merged with the contours of the site. To the north of the proscenium theater, a central foyer connects the rehearsal rooms, faculty studios and practice rooms, offices and libraries. This grouping encourages interaction between theater, dance, and music groups. The main instructional area is separated from the more public proscenium theater, so that university and public functions may occur independently. Both music and theater spaces open to views of the surrounding landscape and campus.

50

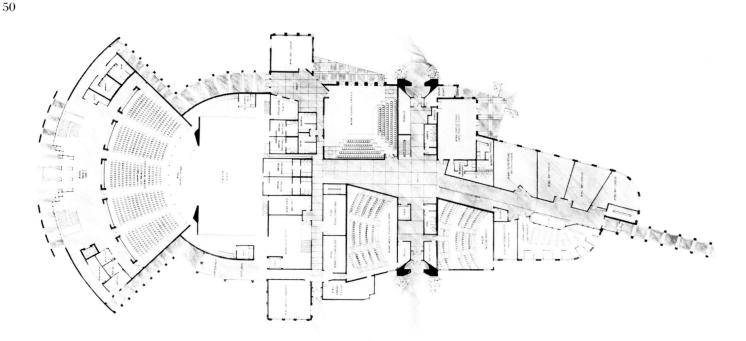

Firm: Cordogan, Clark & Associates
Project Team: John Clark and John Cordogan, with principals Greg Reid, Therese Thompson, and K.C. Lin.

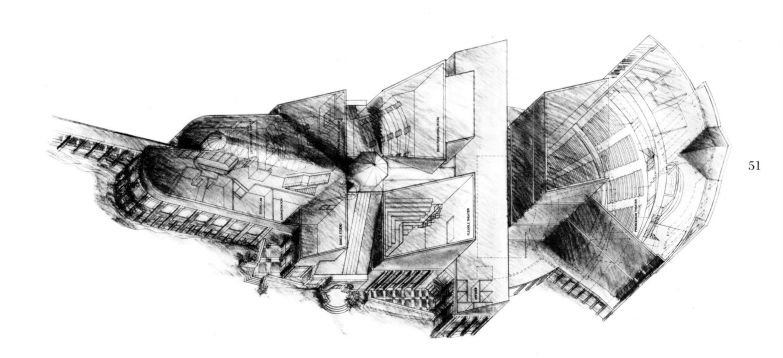

Dirk W. Danker

A principal of Nagle, Hartray & Associates, Ltd., he received a bachelor of architecture from the University of Illinois at Chicago in 1974.

His work has won an AIA Honor Award, has frequently been published, and is in the collection of the Art Institute of Chicago. Several years ago Mr. Danker was one of the winners in the Chicago Architectural Club's Tops Competition.

South 40 Student Housing
Washington University, St. Louis

These dormitories for 400 Washington University students were designed as walk-ups and apartments adjacent to the main campus. Two interlocking buildings, each five stories high, contain 332 units with the community spaces on the lower levels. Their entries open to the downhill terrace and are protected by circular porches. There are 64 apartments in a third building angled at ninety degrees. Each floor has a kitchen, a laundry, study carrels, and accommodations for a resident assistant. Since student government operates on a floor by floor basis, the internal hierarchy of the buildings facilitates the necessary vertical and horizontal connections to other student clusters.

The exteriors are dark red iron-spot brick with Missouri granite lintels, sills and string courses recalling the main quadrangle in scale and materials, and blending with the neighboring dormitories. Vaulted roofs over the living room tiers articulate the facades along with deep-set windows. Rubble granite walks and terraces reinforce the connection to the meandering character of the campus landscape.

52

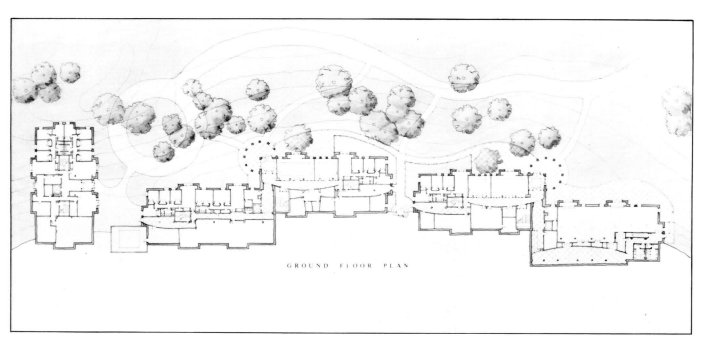

GROUND FLOOR PLAN

Design Architects: Nagle, Hartray & Associates, Ltd.
Architects of Record: Hastings & Chivetta Architects, Inc.
Staff: James Nagle, Dirk W. Danker, and d'Andre Willis.

VIEW FROM SOUTH

NORTH ELEVATION

53

Vladimir G. Donchik

La Rabida Children's Hospital is located on a peninsula in Lake Michigan which was created as part of Olmsted's design for the Columbia Exposition of 1892. The hospital's three buildings, erected at different times, extend along the lakefront. Our project includes the mechanical plant and the Child's Center, which is a place of play and relaxation before children return to the outer world.

The new structure is a focal point on the axis of symmetry which unifies the overall composition. The existing hospital is connected by a bridge to the new Child's Center. We tried to make environmental forms for handicapped children to use, rather than just meeting handicapped requirements. Thus the ramp at the south end of the Child's center turns into a playground, where flower beds raised above the grid and elevated sand and water tables provide therapeutic play for handicapped children.

54

An associate with Vickrey/Ovresat/Awsumb Associates, Inc., he received a master of architecture degree from the Engineering Construction Institute, Leningrad, USSR, in 1971. He has lectured on the history of architecture at Beloit College, the University of Chicago, and the Chicago Architecture Foundation.

He received a commendation in the Logan Square Townhouse Competition in 1980 and won first place in the First International Outhouse Competition sponsored by Archetype *in 1981. He was a finalist in "A Doll's House International Competition" in London in 1982 and was one of ten winners of the "Tops" Competition in 1983. In 1987-1988 he won a limited design-build competition for a residential tower for the Church of the Ascension in Chicago. His work has been exhibited in galleries including the Royal Institute of British Architects, Sotheby's in London, and the Art Institute of Chicago. It has been published in* Progressive Architecture, Architectural Design, Chicago Architecture Annual, *and* Archetype.

Central Mechanical Plant and Child Center
La Rabida Children's Hospital, Chicago, Illinois

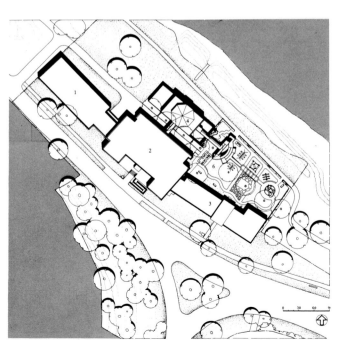

Firm: Vickrey Ovresat Awsumb Associates Incorporated
Staff: Vladimir G. Donchik with Percy Roberts, Joseph Stypka, Gary Green, and Robin Savage.

Paul Florian

*A partner in Florian-Wierzbowski Architecture, P.C., he received
a bachelor of architecture from Washington University, a
diploma from the A.A. in London, and a master of architecture
from the University of Illinois at Chicago. Mr. Florian worked
with Sir Robert Matthew at Johnson-Marshall and Partners in
London from 1973 to 1975, and at Holabird & Root from 1979
to 1981. He has taught at the University of Illinois at Chicago,
and has been a visiting critic, juror, and lecturer at Harvard,
Yale, Notre Dame and the A.A. He co-authored an
article on exhibit design published in* Threshold, *and co-edited
the catalog for the Museum of Science and Industry's exhibit
entitled* 150 Years of Chicago Architecture.

*His buildings and exhibit designs have won several awards from
the Chicago Chapter of the AIA, the "1986 Retail Design of the
Year" from* Interiors *magazine, and two awards from* Industrial
Design *magazine in 1987. His work has been exhibited in
Chicago, London, and Paris, and has been published in*
Architectural Digest, Town and Country, Progressive
Architecture, Interiors *magazine,* The New York Times, *and*
Vogue Decoration.

56

The Amerika-Gedenkbibliothek
Berlin

Our project for the limited competition to design a joint
German-American Library reflects the united, heterogeneous,
and progressive aspects of contemporary West Germany. A
harmonious ensemble of volumes is lashed together by
interpenetrating roofs and walls, symbolizing the triumph of
unity. Walls, sometimes used to divide, are transformed into
symbols of this unification. The engraved Wall of Authors
defines the center of the new library while tying the new and
old parts together along with a system of ramps. The open
stacks are shifted in section and linked to the reading rooms
with a ramp, increasing the interior's openness. A Fountain of
Words creates words of water which float in mid-air before
disappearing into a shallow pool. The curve of the new
Blucherplatz produces a focus for new neighborhood markets
and fairs, in addition to parking. The monumental entrance
enfronts the north-south passage between East and West
Berlin.

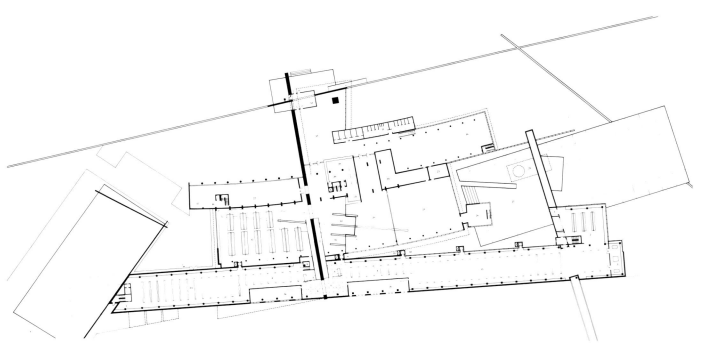

Firm: Florian-Wierzbowski
*Staff: Paul Florian, Steven Wierzbowski, William Worn, Ted Theodore
and Anthony Hurtig*

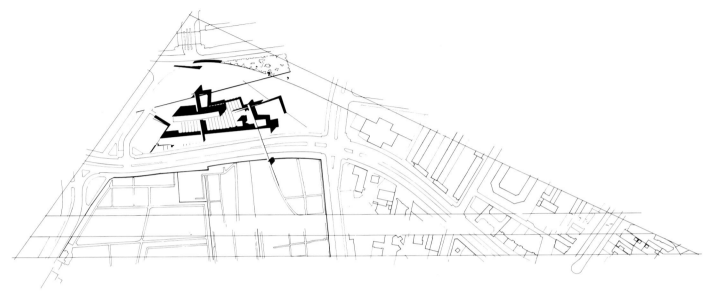

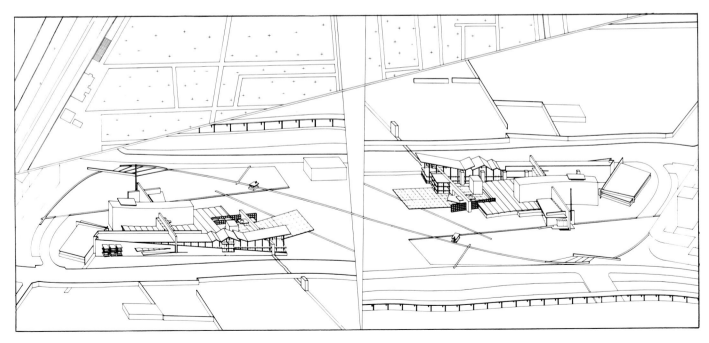

Model: Michael Ambrose, Daniel Marshall, and Ted Theodore
Photography: John Frangoulis
Translation: Christopher Manfrey

Peter E. Frisbee

Northwestern University is expanding and consolidating its communication-media program in a facility adjacent to the Theater and Interpretation Center and the Dance Center. The facility, shared by the journalism and speech departments, will house media studios, lecture rooms, editing rooms, and ancillary spaces. The program requires extensive acoustical treatment, low velocity air supply for the studios, and very little natural light.

The parti is divided in two. One part, adjacent to the existing Theater and Interpretation Center scene shop and service area, holds the studios with mechanical and preparation rooms between them. The adjacent Dance Center relies on natural ventilation, so existing windows could not be blocked. The second part with the remaining program areas is a two-story section rotated relative to the studio section, forming a two-story skylit space that contains the main stair. This space is the place for student-faculty interaction. The junction of these two components is the entry, with a glass-enclosed student lounge and supporting column that give the facility its identity.

58

A project designer with Loebl Schlossman & Hackl, he received degrees from Harvard University and Cornell University, and a doctorate in physics from the University of Maryland in 1972. He has worked at C.F. Murphy and Associates from 1977 to 1980, and Schmidt Garden & Erikson from 1981 to 1983. He was principal in the firm Frisbee/Hirschman Architects during 1983.

His work has been exhibited at the Prairie Avenue Bookshop and the ArchiCenter, and he received honorable mention in the Friends of Downtown-sponsored design competition for Quincy Court. He attended the urban design workshop at the International Academy of Architecture, Sofia, Bulgaria, in May 1988.

Northwestern Studio Building
Evanston, Illinois

SECOND FLOOR PLAN
Scale 1/16" 1'-0"

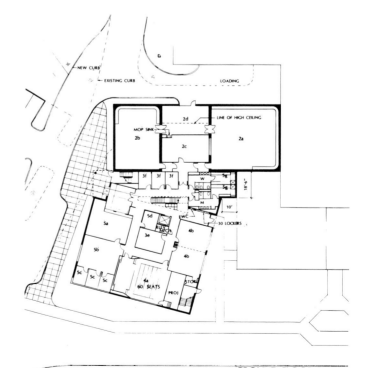

GROUND FLOOR PLAN

Firm: Loebl Schlossman & Hackl
Staff: Donald Hackl, Principal in charge; Jim Pritchett, project manager; Peter Frisbee, Designer.

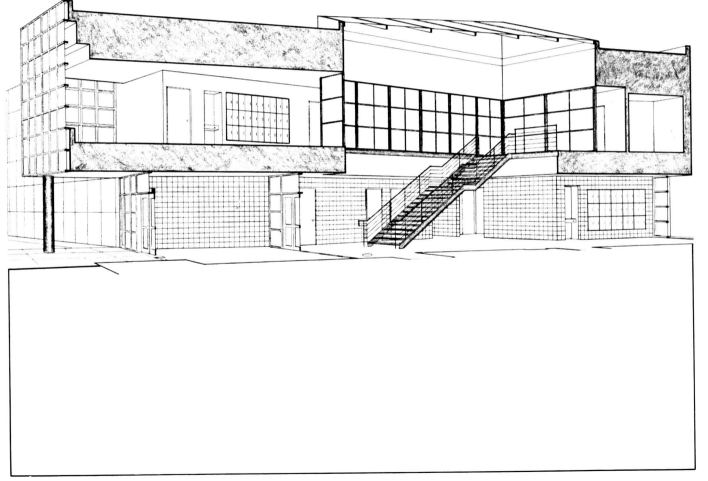

Team: Imre Langmar, Mark Miszuk, Jamie Rodriguez, Frank Weisz,
John Pawlikowski, and Jun Gamundoy.

James Goettsch

The original Bard College Library Building was built in the Greek Revival Style in 1893 as a single skylit room without windows, with three levels of open stacks overlooking the reading room. An unfortunate 1962 addition eliminated the entrance through the portico and destroyed the spatial quality of the main reading room by adding an intermediate floor. Our project will increase the library's size by 150%, recapture the dignity and presence of the original entrance, and provide a harmonious transition to an addition which has a similar presence and dignity, but with an uncompromised modern vocabulary.

The book stacks and studies will be in the proposed addition, which has a 3-story space with clerestory windows that will be the central organizing element. The central space ends with a 4-story circular stair rising to a single room on top, which is an all glass study lounge that looks out into the Hudson River Valley.

60

Mr. Goettsch is a partner in DeStefano/Goettsch, Ltd., and a Fellow of the AIA. He has 18 years of experience with Murphy/ Jahn, 10 of them as a vice president. For 5 years, beginning in 1983, he was executive vice president in charge of the Murphy/ Jahn office in New York City, directly supervising the design of local buildings and several design competitions and proposals.

He has been involved in all phases of the design and construction of more than 20 major buildings and numerous interiors projects located throughout the United States and overseas. He has worked on a wide variety of building types, including high-rise and low-rise office buildings, residential apartment buildings, long span structures (arenas and convention centers), health care facilities, including the design of the world's tallest building for Donald Trump.

Firm: DeStefano/Goettsch, Ltd.
Staff: James Goettsch, James R. DeStefano, Gregory DeStefano, Greg Randall, Larry Saint Germain

61

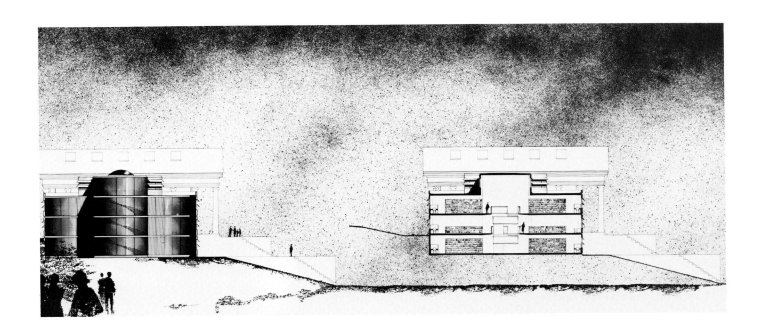

Myron Goldsmith

Myron Goldsmith is both an architect and structural engineer, and has worked in both fields. He is a retired General Partner of Skidmore Owings & Merrill, and a Professor at the Illinois Institute of Technology, where he advises graduate students on their theses. He has been widely published, and a comprehensive book on his work and ideas was published by Rizzoli in 1987.

Williamsburg Suspension Bridge Replacement
New York

Program: Main span 1600 feet, side spans 596 feet, vertical clearance 169 feet; 6 vehicular lanes, 3 subway tracks; and pedestrian and bicycle paths, resulting in a deck 194 feet wide. The new bridge would occupy the same position as the existing bridge.

Solution: A suspension bridge with diagonal stiffening cables and towers of four pylons braced together with cables. The existing anchorages and foundations are reused. The cables are pre-fabricated wire ropes which can be replaced without interrupting traffic. The deck is a stiffened steel plate with a wearing surface. The bridge would be built in two longitudinal halves on either side of the existing bridge. Upon completion, traffic is rerouted, the existing bridge is demolished, and the two halves of the new bridge are slid together and connected without a major interruption of traffic. This entry received one of the three equal awards selected from among the twenty-one entries submitted to the international competition.

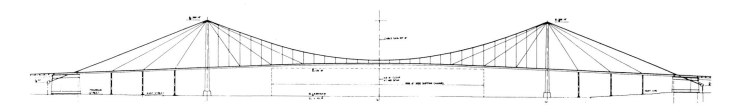

Engineering: Walther and Mory Engineer, Basel; and Schlaich and Partner, Stuttgart, Engineer of Record.

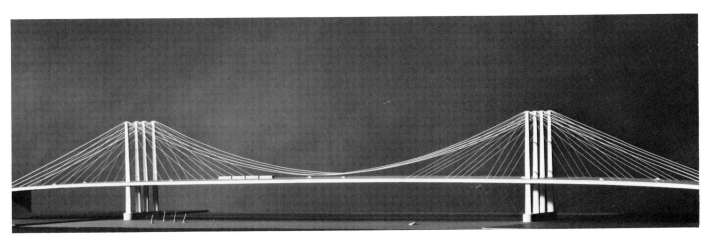

*Design: Myron Goldsmith, Chicago; and Ackermann and Partner,
Stuttgart, architectural consultants.*

Bruce J. Graham

A design partner of Skidmore, Owings & Merrill, Mr. Graham received a bachelor of architecture from the University of Pennsylvania in 1948. He is a Fellow of the AIA, a trustee of the Urban Land Institute, a director of the Urban Land Research Foundation, an honorary trustee of the Institute of Urbanism and Planning of Peru, a trustee and chairman of the Board of Overseers of the School of Fine Arts at the University of Pennsylvania, a board member of the Temple Hoyne Buell Center for American Architecture at Columbia, and a trustee of the Art Institute of Chicago, the Museum of Contemporary Art, and WTTW.

His work has been honored with over seventy awards including National and local AIA Honor Awards, and a design award from Progressive Architecture *magazine. His Inland Steel Building is an officially commissioned Chicago Landmark. A monograph on his work was published in July by Rizzoli.*

Ludgate
London, England

The Ludgate project, consisting of three office buildings, is located on Seacoal Lane behind Old Bailey in the historic heart of London. The narrow and irregular site for Ludgate was reclaimed from the raised tracks of a suburban railway, which were relocated below ground. This new tunnel in turn became the primary axis for the grid which is emphatically expressed in the steel frame structure of each building, organizing the entire project. Newly developed fire-rated glass allows the steel to be expressed directly without fireproofing, and the panelized window wall can be set in back or in front of the structural grid, thus emphasizing it. At ground level each building has a pedestrian arcade with retail components. The three office buildings are linked by a plaza which extends to the buildings bordering the site, creating a pedestrian precinct in place of the former barrier of the railway viaduct.

64

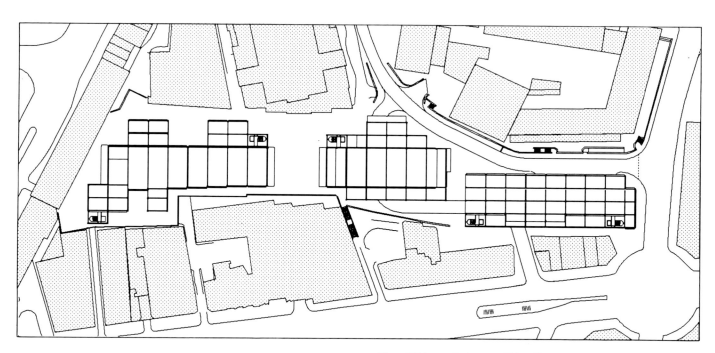

Firm: Skidmore Owings and Merrill
Staff: Bruce J. Graham, design partner; Alan D. Hinklin, partner in charge; George Efstathiou, project manager

*Team: John Burcher, Susan Conger-Austin, Michael Karlovitz, Anwar
Hakim, Madelyn Lee, Stephen Miller, Michel Mossessian, Andrew
Myren, Sae Oh, and Michael Silver.*

Kevin Kemp

Kevin Kemp received his degrees in architecture from the University of Wisconsin at Milwaukee, where he graduated with highest honors in 1982. Before becoming a partner in Decker and Kemp, he was a senior designer with Skidmore, Owings and Merrill. He has taught at Miami University of Ohio and the University of Wisconsin at Milwaukee, and he is a board member of the Newhouse Architecture Competition.

His student work won the Chicago Award, and he led a team which won the Cincinnati Hillside Housing Competition. Recently he won third place in a national competition for the planning and design of a public recreational island in Boston Harbor.

Northbrook Village Hall
Northbrook, Illinois

This new civic structure includes 25,000 square feet on two levels for the departments and services of the Village, the Village Board Room, and the public areas required for other programs and activities. The architecture is traditional, constructed of masonry and stone, with steep roofs, broad arches, and a central stair tower. Because the building's expression is rooted in the regional and traditional architecture of the Village of Northbrook, we hope it will be meaningful as well as beautiful and durable. It should become the central focus of the community's civic life, a symbol of their common purpose, providing a sense of permanence and identity in a rapidly changing physical environment.

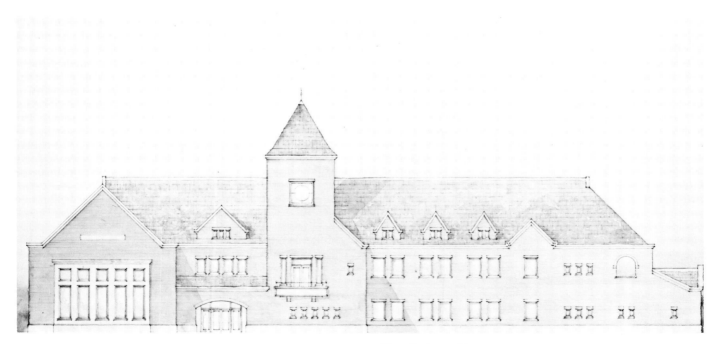

Firm: Decker and Kemp
Staff: Kevin Kemp, Tom Cune

Ronald A. Krueck

A principal in Krueck & Olsen Architects, Ronald Krueck received his bachelor of architecture from the Illinois Institute of Technology in 1970. He worked for C.F. Murphy Associates and Hammond Beeby and Associates. He has taught at IIT, Harvard, and the University of Illinois at Chicago. His work in association with Keith Olsen has received several AIA awards, and has been published and exhibited throughout the United States and Europe. In 1986 he was selected as one of "40 Under 40" architects by the Architectural League of New York.

The Amerika-Gedenkbibliothek
Berlin

As well as an addition to the library, our proposal for this limited competition stresses off-site planning, reflecting our concern for the integrity of this significant area of Berlin. Radiating from the new Blucherplatz are walks and views of the nearby church, and access to a new entrance to the cemetery, The original facade is retained, and the new facilities are arranged to allow access to the existing building and surrounding points of interest off the Blucherplatz. Preserving the original building's identity, the new building involves the sculpted form of a new auditorium, and punctured planes of the cafeteria walls across the front of the complex.

Firm: Krueck and Olsen, Architects

Internally, the cutting of the vault provides a transitional entry to the core. A spiral stair is a vertical focus on axis with the church to the east and the restored path to the cemetery. The circulation zone is a transparent shaft which slices the floors and projects towards the church, with a glass ramp enclosure connecting each level. The concrete structural grid is shifted in response to the site, and the glass curtain wall is articulated with different colors, responding to the library stack module. Perforated metal wings deflect the north view and screen the library space from public activity in the plaza.

Michael Lustig

Originally constructed as a single family residence, Central Synagogue is located on the near north side of Chicago in a turn-of-the-century neoclassical building. The program calls for the restoration of the existing 3000 sq.ft. facility, and an addition of 6000 sq.ft. for a sanctuary and meeting spaces.

The structural steel frame is sheathed with limestone blocks and forms the exterior wall enclosure. Vaulted plaster ceilings are suspended between the steel beams, and the steel columns are enclosed with plaster, stone, laminate, and steel ornament. The symmetrical sanctuary space begins with an entry that is connected to the main entrance of the building by a suspended vaulted canopy and terminates with the arc.

70

Michael Lustig was educated at Ohio State University, Cornell University, and the University of Illinois, where he received a master of architecture degree in 1974. He is a principal of Michael Lustig & Associates, and previously he was a research assistant for the U.S. Defense Department. He has lectured at Ohio State University, and has taught at the University of Illinois at Chicago. He edited volumes 5, 6, and 7 of the Chicago Architectural Journal.

He received several awards from the Chicago Chapter AIA, including a Young Architect Award in 1988, as well as a Gold Medal from the Illinois Masonry Council. His work has been in numerous exhibitions, including shows at the Art Institute, the Museum of Science and Industry, the Merchandise Mart, and several galleries and schools of architecture. He was recently included in the "99 Chicago Architects" exhibit at the Gulbenkian Foundation in Lisbon.

Central Synagogue
Chicago, Illinois

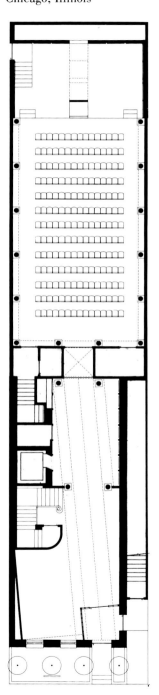

Firm: Michael Lustig and Associates
Staff: Atul Karkhanis and Samuel Assefa

Andrew Metter

A senior designer with Perkins & Will, he received a master of architecture degree from Washington University in 1976. He was formerly a principal in the firm of Lubotsky, Metter, Worthington & Law. He received a Chicago Chapter AIA Young Architect Award in 1985.

His work has received design awards from Progressive Architecture *magazine and the Architectural League of New York, and a number of Distinguished Building Awards from the Chicago Chapter AIA. It has been exhibited at the Walker Art Center, Minneapolis, the Art Institute of Chicago, and the Museum of Science and Industry.*

Sangamon State University Health Sciences Building
Springfield, Illinois

This project is for the design of a 56,000 square foot Health Sciences Building for Sangamon State University in Springfield, Illinois. The program called for university-wide computer facilities and faculty offices below grade, with two levels of chemistry and biology laboratories above. The L-shaped courtyard scheme should minimize circulation and create a community feeling. The courtyard was excavated to bring light and ventilation to the lower level.

The major program elements were expressed in massing and elevation, with laboratories developed as masonry blocks with strip windows. The offices were given a glass curtainwall, the triangular electron microscope suite got its own structure to isolate vibration, and the biology department's green house was developed as a glass pyramid on the south side of the building.

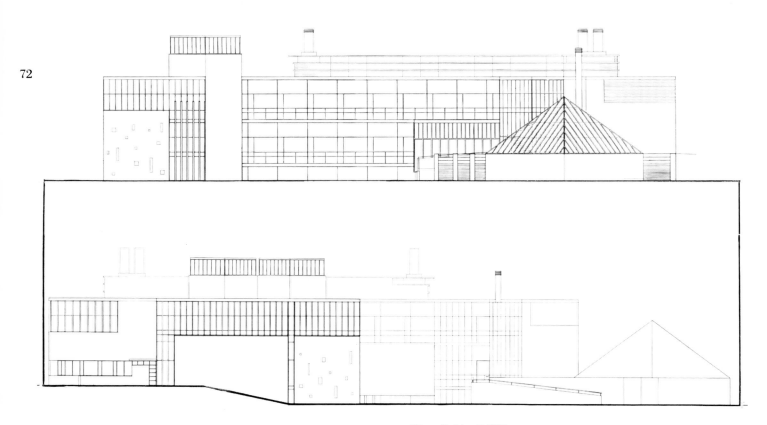

Firm: Perkins & Will
Staff: Andrew Metter with Peter Tham and Joseph Chronister
Model: Peter Tham and Michael Stutz

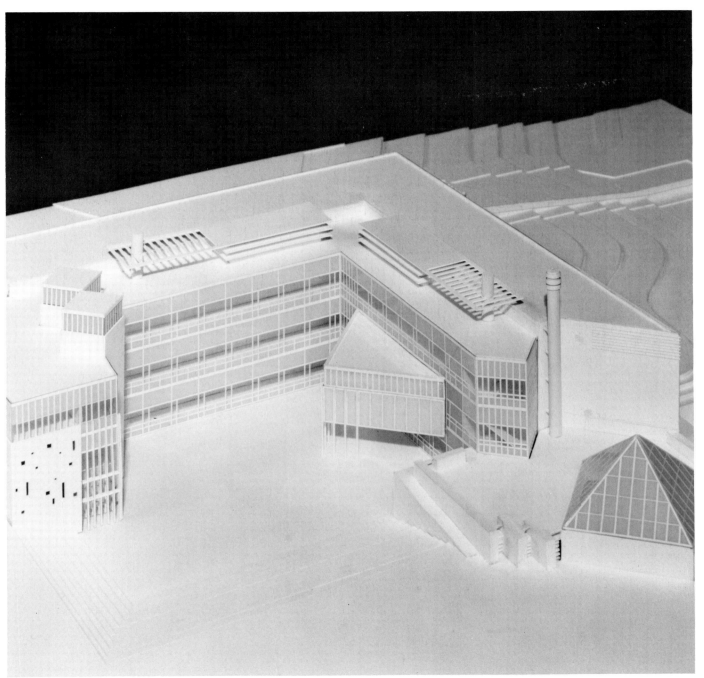

Linda Lee Nelson

Hopewell Center
Anderson, Indiana

Historically, handicapped people have been segregated or anonymously dispersed in low-rent locations throughout the city. Preschoolers have been lumped with adults, creating confusion for both clients and staff. The research and development behind our design for the Hopewell Center evolved philosophically around our desire to provide a place of value for previously devalued citizens. Set amidst seven acres of midwestern cornfield, the 50,000 square foot campus is a reaffirmation and celebration of the right of all people to have pride in their place of learning.

The identity and function of the center emanate from the archetypal home in the center of the campus. It serves the 250 clients and 70 staff as a programmatic and social center for the activities which prepare them for eventual acceptance within the community. The administration building, with its greeting spaces, meeting porches, and offices, frames the campus behind a tree-ringed drive. A canopied walk connects to the preschool education building with its play yard on one side, and the adult education building with picnic area on the other. Beyond the classrooms are the multi-use gymnasium with a cafeteria shared by adults and preschoolers, and the work education building.

A partner of Keane Nelson Keane, architects and animators, Ms. Nelson received her bachelor of science in environmental design, and her bachelor of architecture from Ball State University in 1978, and was awarded the AIA school medal. In 1979 she traveled to Turkey as a Fulbright Hays Scholar. In 1984, she received her master of architecture degree from the University of Illinois at Chicago.

She has taught at Ball State University, at the University of Illinois at Chicago, and at the University of Illinois / SAIC summer Versailles program. She is an Associate Professor and currently Head of the Department of Interior Architecture at the School of the Art Institute of Chicago. She is a member of the AIA, Classical America, and the National Institute for Architectural Education.

Firm: Keane Nelson Keane Architects
Associated architect: Taylor Architects, Inc.

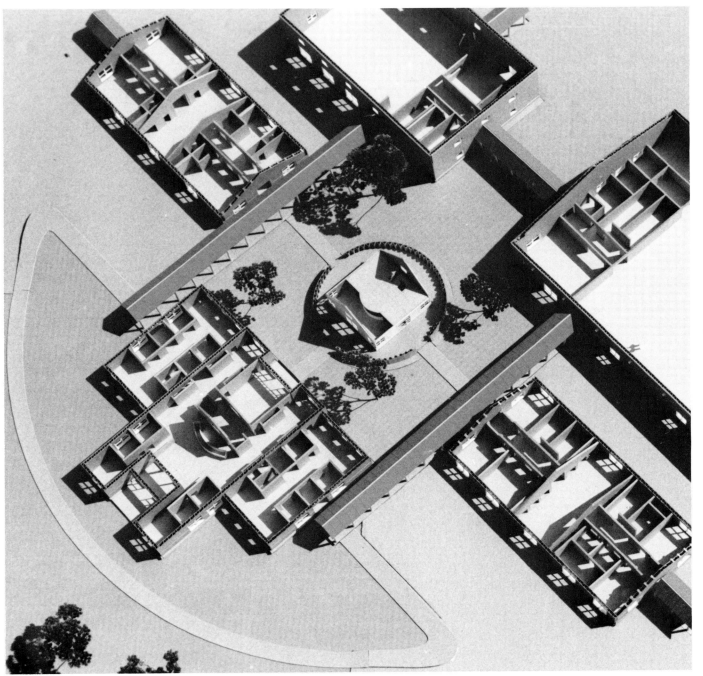

Thomas Norman Rajkovich

In private practice in Evanston, Mr. Rajkovich received his bachelor of architecture magna cum laude from the University of Notre Dame in 1983. With David T. Mayernik, he won the International Competition for the Completion of the Capitol Grounds in Saint Paul, Minnesota, including five Capitol precinct bridges. In 1988 he won a Faculty Award for Design Excellence from the Association of Collegiate Schools of Architecture. In 1987 he received the Arthur Ross Award from Classical America, an award from the Minnesota Chapter of the American Society of Landscape Architects, and special mention in the Chicago Bar Association's "New Voices, New Visions" Exhibit. In 1985 he won the Burnham Prize from the Chicago Architectural Club. His work has been exhibited in Rome, Chicago, New York, San Francisco, Minneapolis and Saint Paul.

He is currently teaching in the Rome program of the University of Notre Dame. He has previously taught at the University of Illinois, and has been a guest critic for the Rhode Island School of Design's Rome program, and the Illinois Institute of Technology.

The Korean War Veterans' Memorial Design Competition
Washington, D. C.

This project is dedicated to the memory of my grandmother, Pauline Zizoff, whose faith offered me eternal hope, and whose life and love will forever be my inspiration.

76

Leslie Ventsch

The parti comprises a chapel and subsidiary sacred spaces, and the secular, administrative office block. Together they define a back yard open on the north to playing fields, and enclosed on the south by a "front porch." This open porch provides a focal point for a new entrance drive into the campus, and the ensemble becomes the focus for the entire campus. The project's massing, materials, and delineation derive from the existing Priests' Villa, which dates from the 1890's. The porch extends the veranda on the Villa, and creates a familial meeting place for this 106 year-old community serving abused and abandoned children.

78

Leslie Ventsch is a design architect with Opus North Corporation, a design-build firm. He has worked with Holabird & Root in Chicago, F.S. Platou in Oslo, Norway, and Mitchell / Giurgola Architects in Philadelphia. In 1986, he won the Chicago Architectural Club's Burnham Prize fellowship to the American Academy in Rome.

A Chapel for Maryville Academy
Des Plaines, Illinois

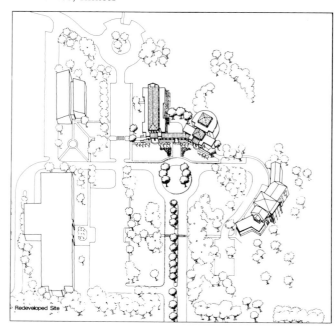

Redeveloped Site

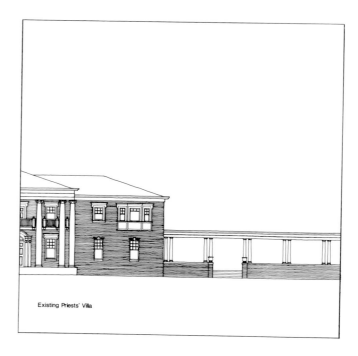

Existing Priests' Villa

Firm: Opus North Corporation
Staff: Leslie Ventsch with Randy Schumacher, Julie Gaudreault, and Daesik Park

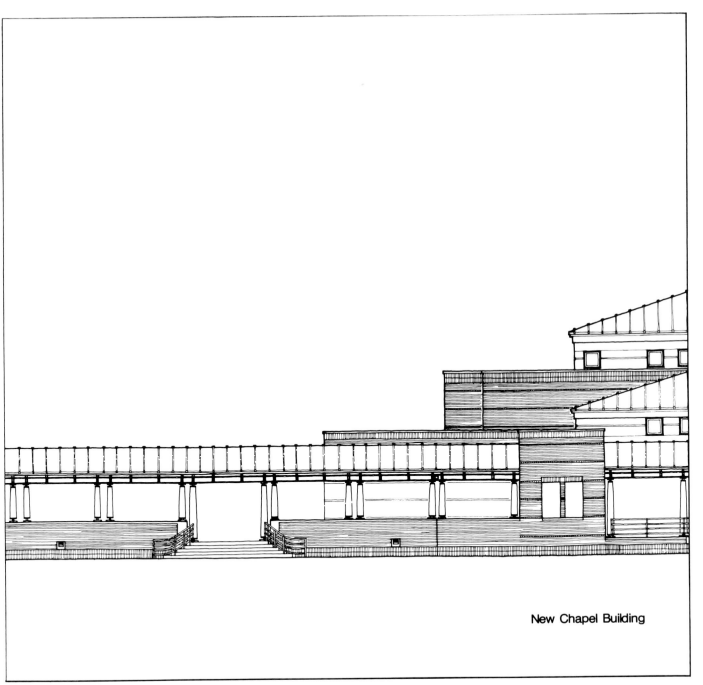

New Chapel Building

Ben Weese

A partner in Weese Hickey Weese, he received both bachelor and master of architecture degrees from Harvard University, and a scholarship and certificate from the Ecole des Beaux-Arts at Fountainebleau. From 1957 to 1977 he was with Harry Weese and Associates. He has been a visiting critic and lecturer at numerous universities including Washington University, St. Louis; Harvard University; and Miami University, Oxford, Ohio.

His work has received numerous awards from the Chicago Chapter AIA, and has appeared in many exhibitions including "Late Entries to the Chicago Tribune Tower Competition," "New Chicago Architecture" at the Museo di Castelvecchio, Verona, and the Chicago Seven.

Fox Valley Evangelical Free Church
Algonquin, Illinois

This Christian Congregation is growing and the building is planned so it can expand in pinwheel fashion. No overt Christian symbolism is desired but a definite, concentrated atmosphere for drama, preaching and music is required. Movement toward and into the structure is stimulated by a series of light sources and offset focuses, entering a cross-axis space and reversing into the main sanctuary on the diagonal. To counteract the blandness of the single level program requirement variations in ceiling heights and light sources are exploited for dramatic effect. The classroom wing is focused on an internal indirect natural light source from an east oriented monitor. Movement into the main sanctuary is under a low balcony then into the rising volume of space spanned by a wooden ridge truss and flanking trusses. Controlled amounts of light enter at a ridge skylight. Thus plan, section and elevation are manipulated to express active present and future asymmetry.

80

Firm: Weese Hickey Weese

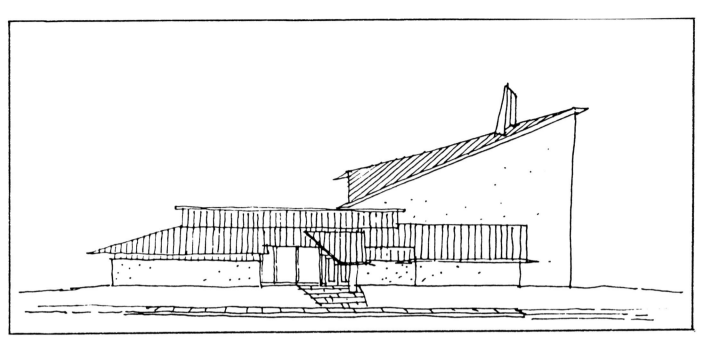

Stephen Yas

This plan was created for 1.5 miles of Fox River promenade around the island which is Aurora's central business district. The goal for the promenade and the guidelines for adjacent development was to create a lively pedestrian circulation system at street level, which would provide a focus for activities and be a catalyst for transforming the downtown into a vital eighteen-hour-a-day city. The design takes advantage of Aurora's traditional values, classic architecture, and historic elements.

The theme for the Foxwalk is an "Historic Town Trail" using landmark buildings and historic sites as a series of "exhibits" highlighting important events in Aurora's development. Aurora was the first city to have electric street lights, sixteen superb 152 feet high towers. The centerpiece of the trail is a replica of one of those lamp towers (Aurora's own 'Eiffel Tower') commemorating Aurora's innovative lead into the modern age of electricity.

82

The director of design at Raymond J. Green & Associates, Mr. Yas received a bachelor of architecture from Ohio University in 1973, and a graduate diploma in urban design from Oxford Polytechnic in England, in 1975. He has worked at The Architects Collaborative in Cambridge, Massachusetts, and at the Ministry of Housing in Israel. He was a senior architect and urban designer at Skidmore, Owings & Merrill from 1977 to 1981, and an Associate and designer with Lohan Associates from 1981 to 1987. A critic and lecturer at Notre Dame and the University of Wisconsin at Milwaukee, he also received an education exchange award to the Moscow Architectural Institute, USSR.

His work has received a Distinguished Building Award from the Chicago Chapter AIA, and HUD's honor award for housing design. He has been published in Architectural Record *and* Inland Architect *and his work has been exhibited in the Art Institute's "New Chicago Architecture" exhibition, and at the University of Notre Dame. He was a Commissioner on the Evanston Plan Commission from 1979 to 1987. Currently he is a member of the Evanston Preservation Committee and serves on the board of directors of Design Evanston.*

Aurora "Foxwalk" Promenade
Aurora, Illinois

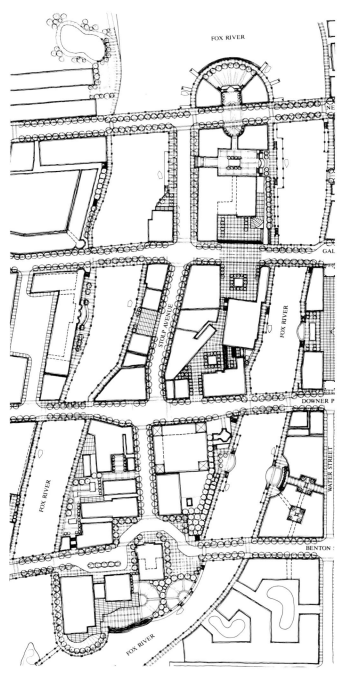

Firm: Raymond J. Green & Associates Architects, Inc.
Staff: Stephen Yas, design; Raymond Green, principal; and Myn Ancheta and Tom Tietz

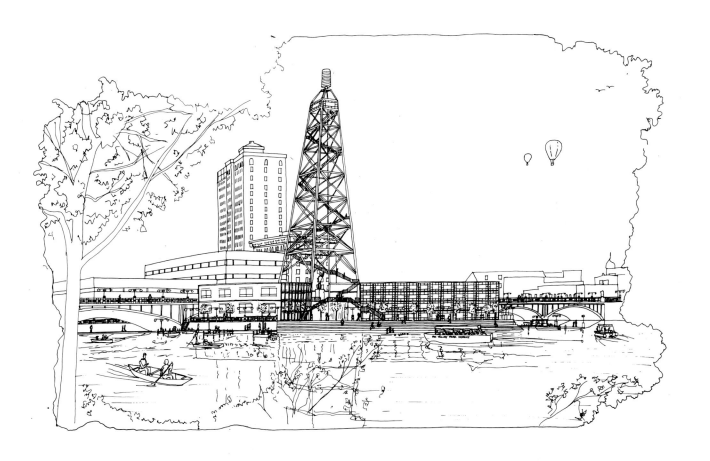

83

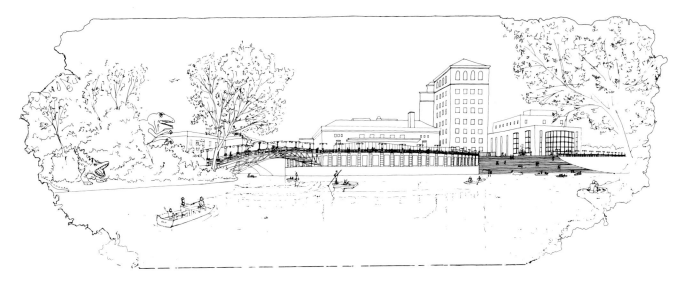

Sidney Robinson

Commercial work for an architect presents the paradox of being allowed to spend money, if the client considers the appearance of the project a generator of revenue, in response to motivations that are a long way from more culturally elevated ideals. Commercial clients can also be frustrating if they dream grand ideas and then want it done with nothing but blue smoke and mirrors. Making a tight fit between form and function, as defined by successful market penetration, suggests a pleasant freedom to cook up a tasty stew of colors, forms, and allusions from a wide range of sources.

But it can all be fun. Or it can be the opportunity to correct the drift into cultural chaos by impacting the market with the diverting look of rectitude. The modern tradition of architecture correcting society makes commercial work difficult. Does one give into a *zeitgeist*, even though one prefers another time and place, or does one struggle to get the cultural train back on track by reminding people what they are missing.

The effort to redeem retail shopping from the crass and the automobile underlies a good bit of current commercial work. Howard Decker's mall in Naperville deftly recalls the North Shore suburbs that Naperville strives to be like. The Lake Forest shopping center by Howard Van Doren Shaw is a close neighbor to this project in spirit and intention. Of course there are differences, and they are the hardest to accommodate. The budget restraint and the current construction technology tend to abbreviate the earlier model. Of course the cars in the parking lot go a lot faster than those in 1915, so the total impression may be the same. Decker has presented once again a reminder of a gentler world in which architecture was not quite so compromised as it seems to be today.

The other alternative is to go with the flow as David Hansen chooses to do with a prototype Turtle Wax Auto Appearance Center. The challenge of a facility enhancing not the operation, but the appearance of the all-consuming destroyer of traditional architecture is to somehow escape architectural history and find a way to embrace this disruptive element. Hansen has produced an image that may reflect the multiple facets of the world seen from a moving car when he might have used the singular image of the car itself whose tightly stretched skin compresses a dazzling object. Shine, curves, reflections all dancing over a compact form have been set aside for an assemblage of modernist forms.

James Law's Ravinia Park Gift Shop is a more familiar project that sets a frame for exposing goods for sale. It is a large show window emphasizing visibility, light, simplicity. The framing planes and columns set up the predictability that any consumer desires, while the gentle deformations of wall and counter invite by their accommodation. The comforting balance between the cold calculation of market profiles, production costs and inventory monitoring and the invitation to individuals who imagine that their personal desires are being responded to directly is happily achieved in this lantern of illusion.

Illusion is also at the heart of Richard Jay Solomon's Lambs Farm Miniature Golf Course and Clubhouse. The farm image, derived, one imagines, not only from the fortuitous client name, but also from a pleasant nostalgia, provides a striking metaphor that can govern a whole range of choices. The delight at finding the alignment between metaphor and mini golf requirements adds to the diversion that motivates the whole project. Solomon has drawn a lot out of this image and has intensified it with illusions cut out of plywood sheets. As a result we have a tight fit, an appropriate image and skillful execution.

The illusion of an older form covering a newer use is a favorite way for architects to avoid the terrible conflict between traditional architecture and contemporary commercial realities. Cynthia Weese, whose sensitivity to the taste of previous eras is well known, takes a generic form of urban construction and adapts it to new uses. The choices of openings, their division and the rearrangement of internal space are made carefully and with considerable effect.

Adaptations are always satisfying because the architect can share the effort with something they were not responsible for. Dan Wheeler's Goose Island Brewery Roof Deck is a wonderful example, recently made high art by Coop Himmelblau in Vienna, of topping a substantial piece of construction with a nautical or aerial fantasy. The light, insectile or avian frames with membranes flying perch on the top of a cliff providing escape and attraction inside and out.

There is not much one can add to David Woodhouse's description of how he added "costume jewelry" to an existing warehouse. It appears that not only his language, but his ornamentation are right on target. Thus we end this review of Chicago Architectural Club members's essays in commercial work with a brilliant example of adjusting to, no, embracing, the new world and enjoying it.

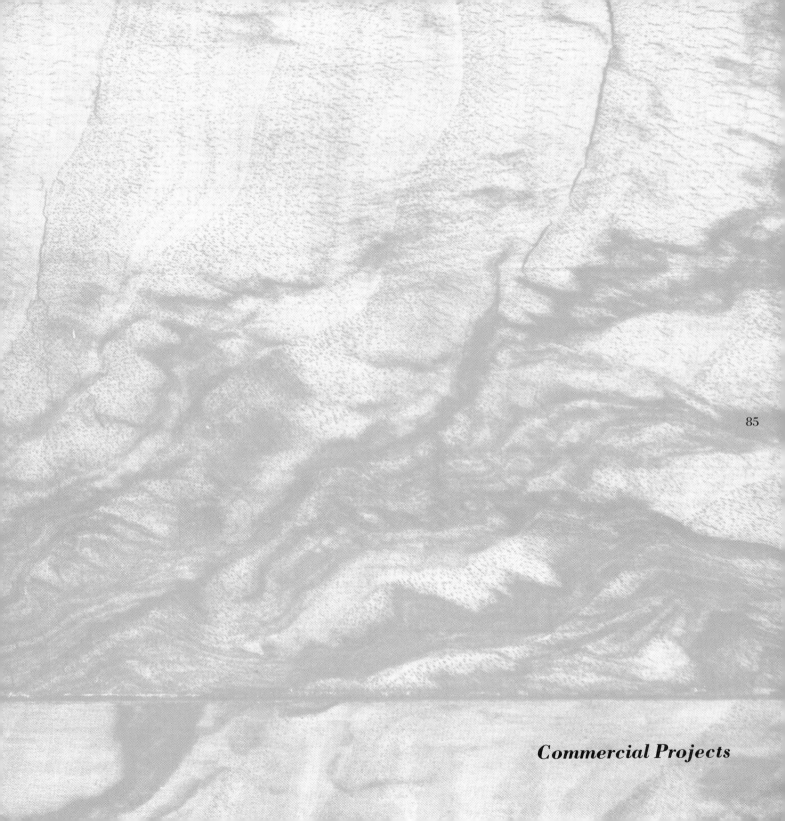

85

Commercial Projects

Howard Decker

Howard Decker received a bachelor of science from Northwestern University in 1972, and a master of architecture from the University of Illinois at Chicago in 1978. Before founding Decker and Kemp, he was an associate partner in Nagle, Hartray and Associates, where he supervised the design and construction of projects such as urban and office campus planning studies, corporate interiors, libraries, and residential projects. He has taught and lectured widely, and is a Contributing Editor for Inland Architect *magazine. He has served as a Vice-Chairman of the Evanston Historic Preservation Commission, and is presently a board member of the Landmarks Preservation Council of Illinois, and the Chicago Architectural Press.*

His work has been exhibited in the Art Institute of Chicago, and published in the Chicago Architectural Journal, *which he also has co-edited. In 1988 he was awarded the Chicago Chapter AIA Young Architect Award.*

A Shopping Center in Naperville
Naperville, Illinois

The site for this 100,000 sq. ft. project is elevated above the intersection of two big roads, so it was important to establish a memorable image. In this environment, one of enormous change and visual competition, we felt it was imperative to re-establish the traditional architectural palette of the surrounding community. In addition, the shopping center needs to make sense at several scales, from the high-speed passer-by, to the pedestrian getting out of the parked car, to the pedestrian next to the building. Our traditional palette of forms adapts easily to this task, through a selection of materials scaled to each distance.

86

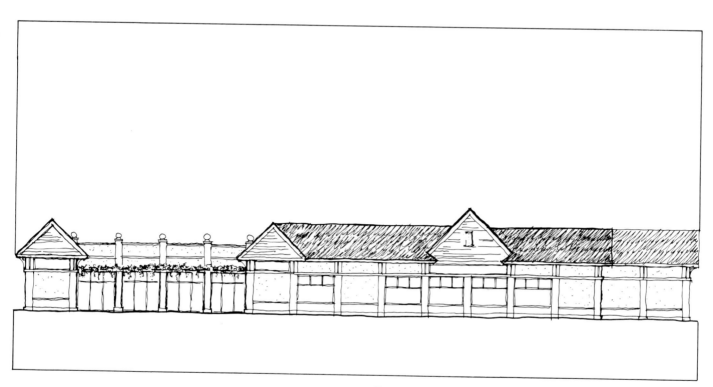

Firm: Decker and Kemp, Architects
Staff: Kevin Kemp, Howard Decker, Doug Ruther

David A. Hansen

Turtle Wax, Inc.'s Auto Appearance Center is a state-of-the-art prototype facility providing both automated car-washing and hand-performed detailing. The project incorporates the latest developments in fine car-washing equipment, integrating both computerized "touchless" pressurized-water equipment and selected friction machinery. The massing and architectural expression of the 15,000-square-foot prototype facility conceptually embody the functional processes contained within the building. The prototype, to be constructed in locations across the country, strives for a state-of-the-art car-wash esthetic consistent with Turtle Wax's reputation for quality products and services.

88

A Vice President and Design Principal of Perkins & Will, he received a bachelor of architecture degree from the University of Illinois at Urbana in 1967. He has worked with the Chicago firms of C.F. Murphy & Associates and Skidmore, Owings & Merrill, and was design principal for PACE, a multi-national firm. He is a member of the Committee on Design and the Practice Committee AIA, the board of directors of the CAAC, and the Planning & Urban Design Committee of the Friends of Downtown. He has served as a visiting critic and lecturer on design at the University of Miami in Ohio, The University of Illinois at Urbana, and Illinois Central University, as well as international conferences for the Bahrain and Kuwait Society of Engineers.

His work has received two Distinguished Building Awards from the Chicago Chapter AIA, and won First Place in three international competitions. His designs have been featured in Inland Architect, Architecture, Progressive Architecture, Building Design & Construction, Interiors, Contract *and the* Chicago Architecture Annual.

Turtle Wax Auto Appearance Center
Preliminary Design for a National Prototype Facility

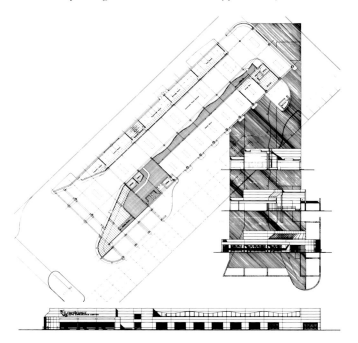

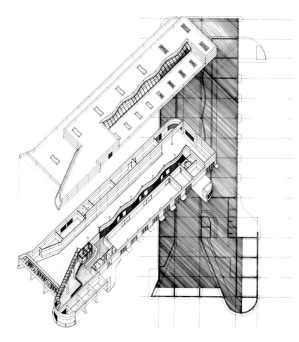

Firm: Perkins & Will
Staff: David A. Hansen with project designer Michael Henthorn

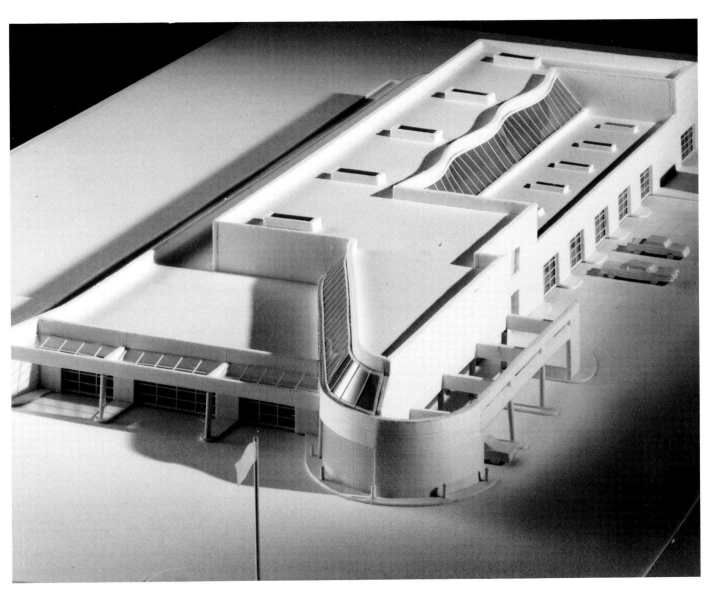

John C. Lahey

Oakbrook Shopping Center is a single story, open air shopping center; expanding the center with a two-level retail addition required a memorable gesture. A curving, white-glazed brick arcade slices through the 675 feet length of the project, simultaneously linking the entrances, generating two open-air courts, and providing a sense of drama. By establishing a connected series of spaces, the arcade mitigates the tunnel-like effect a building of this length would have, and constantly refers the shopper to new viewpoints as storefronts come into view. Opposite the smooth, curved wall is a highly geometric arcade to which vertical transportation elements are linked. These small structures, rendered in steel and glass, are intended to be jewel-like fragments in the over-all scheme. The materials are all unusually light-responsive, especially at night when they collect and reflect light from the shops.

90

A partner with Solomon Cordwell Buenz & Associates, he received a bachelor of architecture from Cornell University in 1976, and has worked for Brenner Danforth Rockwell and Murphy/Jahn.

Oakbrook Center Expansion III
Oak Brook, Illinois

Staff: Frank Balnius, Tom Humes, John Lahey, Jacek Lazarczyk, Vern Lohman, Michel Lough, Carol Lowry, Janet Quevedo, Steve Rybicki, Al Silinis

Firm: Solomon Cordwell Buenz & Associates
Owner: Oakbrook Urban Venture

James Law

This new structure replaced an obsolete wood souvenir shop at Ravinia. Relocated to the back side of the 1902 Murray Theater, where it is visible to both pavilion and lawn audiences, it triples the size of the original shop.

By day, the shop is a minimal and abstract composition set against a large neutral wall. The horizontal roof with deep overhangs, the exposed structure, and the large expanses of glass capture the light and airy feeling characteristic of the tall oak trees and leafy canopies at Ravinia. At night the shop transforms into a volume of light, highlighting the structure, the display kiosk, the counter and the storage wall. The roof canopy, which provides a shield from sun and rain during the day, and emits a warm glow of light at night for both illumination and dramatic effect. The materials are clear glass, gray steel, gold aluminum, oak panels, black granite and cream-colored stucco.

92

A project designer with Ullman & Fill, Architects, Mr. Law received his bachelor of architecture from Cornell University in 1977. Previously he was a principal designer with Lubotsky, Metter, Worthington & Law, Architects. He has taught at the University of Wisconsin at Milwaukee.

His work has received a Distinguished Building Award from the Chicago Chapter AIA, has been exhibited at the Art Institute, the Museum of Science and Industry, and the Archicenter, and has been published by the AIA Journal, the New Art Examiner, and Inland Architect. In 1985 and 1987 he was honored by the Chicago Bar Association in its juried selection of work by young architects.

Ravinia Park Gift Shop
Highland Park, Illinois

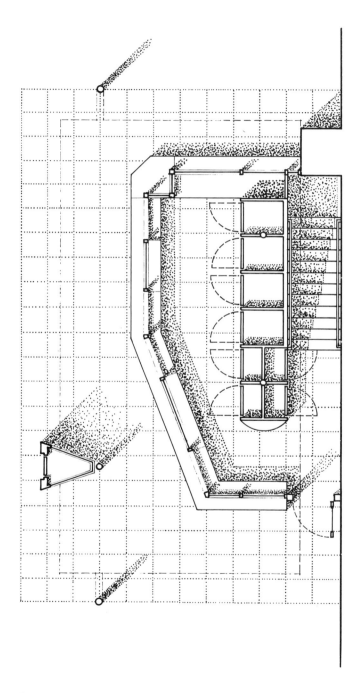

Firm: Lubotsky, Metter, Worthington and Law

93

Richard Jay Solomon

Principal of Richard Jay Solomon & Associates, he received his bachelor of architecture from the Massachusetts Institute of Technology in 1967 and a master of environmental design from Yale in 1969. He has worked for Solomon Cordwell Buenz and Associates and the Department of Planning of the City of Chicago. He has been a visiting critic at numerous universities including Massachusetts Institute of Technology, Kansas University, and the University of Illinois at Urbana. For the last five years he has taught at the University of Illinois in Chicago.

His work has been exhibited in several group exhibitions, and is in the Department of Architecture collection of the Art Institute of Chicago. His work and articles have been published in Inland Architect, Architectural Forum, Architecture, Threshold, Archetype, *and* Cricket *magazine for children.*

Lambs Farm Miniature Golf Course and Clubhouse
Libertyville, Illinois

The Lambs, Inc. provides vocational, residential and social support services for mentally handicapped adults. In addition to small business and family attractions, Lambs Farm desired a miniature golf course and clubhouse. Our solution attempts to transcend the typical commercial examples of this recreational type by developing a farm-theme play environment. The use of farm elements, abstracted in plywood, or outlined in structure, emphasizes both the playfulness and the character of the composition.

94

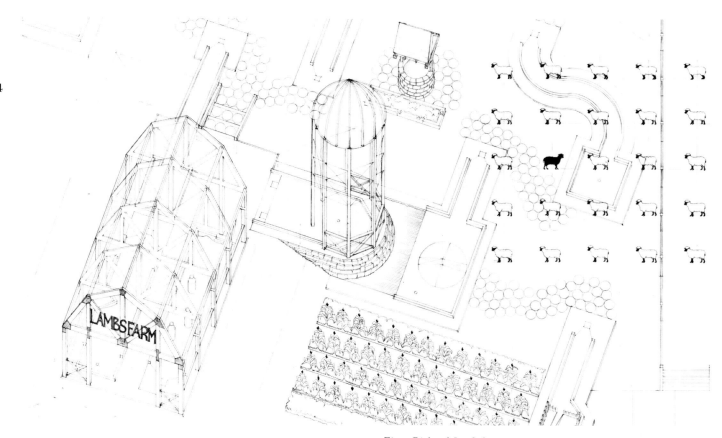

Firm: Richard Jay Solomon
Staff: Richard Jay Solomon with Ruth Olin and Frances Andrews

Cynthia Weese

A crumbling coach house, its overgrown garden, and an 1890's commercial / apartment building have been integrated into a commercial garden center. The coach house has been completely remodeled, with new 'old' windows rescued from a 1930's Deco building, and new French doors opening into the garden. A dramatic asymmetrical stair adds necessary counterpoint to the symmetries in plan and elevation. The garden has become an outdoor room, defined by a canopy of leaves, and pergolas, trellises, and paving, with a bit of a twist. The palette of materials is industrial: galvanized ribbed siding on the penthouse, stamped metal fencing, brushed concrete flooring on one level, and rough-sawn cedar on another. Galvanized gutter stock surrounds fluorescent tubes, and stamped metal forms incandescent sconces. These materials respond to the character of the existing building, and of the business itself, while providing a refreshing contrast to the inherent romanticism of the garden plants.

96

A partner in Weese Hickey Weese, she received a bachelor of architecture from Washington University in 1965. She has worked at Harry Weese and Associates, and has been in private practice. She has been a visiting critic and lecturer at universities including Washington University, Miami University of Ohio, the University of North Carolina, Notre Dame University, the University of Wisconsin, and Mississippi State University. She has been the president of the Chicago Chapter AIA and the AIA Foundation, and co-edited the catalog 150 years of Chicago Architecture, *published by the Museum of Science and Industry.*

Her work has won Distinguished Building Awards and Interior Design Awards from the AIA, which also awarded her its Service Award for organizing the exhibit Chicago Women in Architecture. *She has exhibited work at the Art Institute of Chicago, the Walker Art Center, the Chicago Historical Society, the Avery Library at Columbia University, and at the Gulbenkian Museum in Lisbon.*

The Secret Garden of a New Leaf
1816 North Wells, Chicago, Illinois

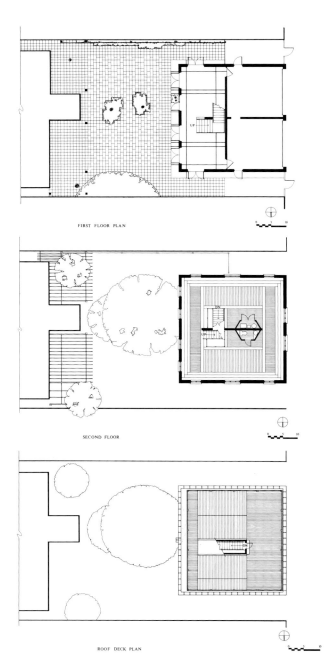

FIRST FLOOR PLAN

SECOND FLOOR

ROOF DECK PLAN

Firm: Weese Hickey Weese Architects, Ltd.
Staff: Cynthia Weese, Richard Klein, Andrew Dresdner

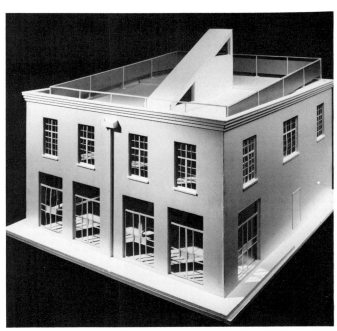

Daniel Harding Wheeler

Perched on the roof of an industrial loft building on Goose Island, the roof deck is an annex to a small brewery located in the building below. The deck is conceived as autonomous, hovering six feet above the existing roof, and connecting to the existing building only with light steel bridges, tension cables and stairs. Dark stained glue-lam beams and inset borders trim the silvery wood floor. An inclined fabric vault, lifted off the floor by tubular steel frames and struts, crowns the composition. By day, the vault provides shelter from the elements. During the evening, the vault distributes diffuse light over the deck and becomes a beacon to the surrounding commercial district.

98

Principal of Daniel Wheeler Architects, he received a bachelor of architecture from the Rhode Island School of Design (Rome) in 1981. Prior to opening his architectural practice in 1987, he was an associate partner and studio head at Skidmore, Owings & Merrill, and was previously associated with Machado Silvetti Architects, Himmel/Bonner, and Hanno Weber and Associates. He recently directed a masters studio at the University of Wisconsin at Milwaukee.

Mr. Wheeler was the recipient of a NEA Traveling Fellowship in 1980, and the AIA Young Architect Award in 1985. His work, which ranges from furniture to entire communities, has won a number of competitions and AIA awards, and has been exhibited and published both nationally and abroad.

Goose Island Brewery Roof Deck
Chicago, Illinois

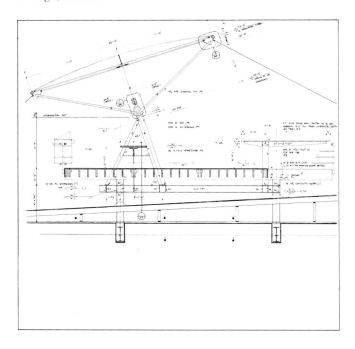

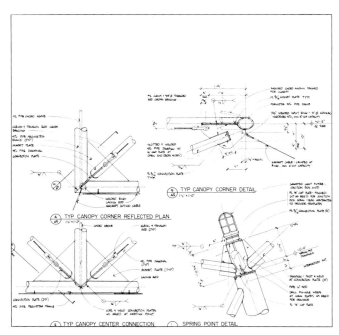

Staff: Lawrence Kearns, with Daniel Wheeler, Liza Bachrach, and Lora Huettenrauch.
Structural Consultants: Stearn/Joglekar

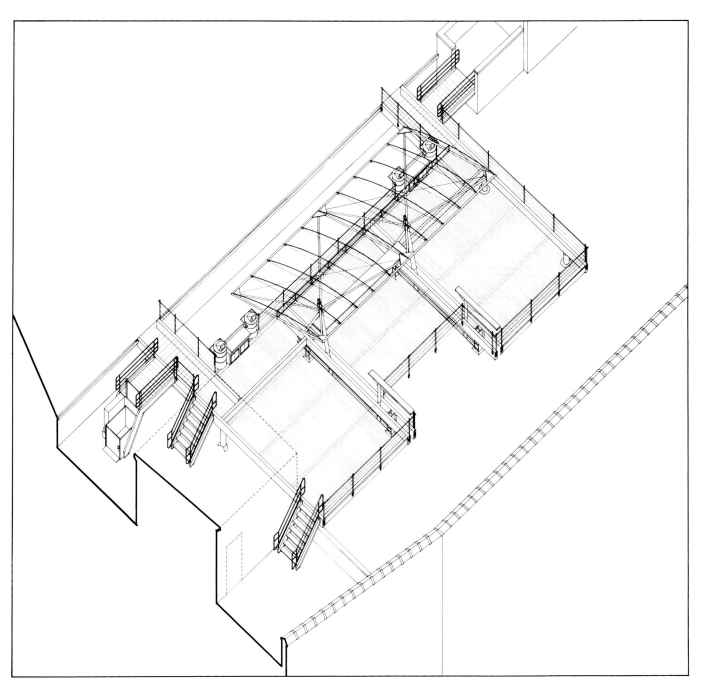

David Woodhouse

407 East 25th Street
Chicago, Illinois

A demi-deco warehouse building is being renovated into an office building by the addition of a set of costume jewelry: a blazing tiara atop the entry tower, and glittering shoulder clips on each corner. These baubles will be constructed of corrugated panels of translucent fiberglass on steel frames, and will be brightly lit from within and below.

100

A partner in Langdon and Woodhouse, Mr. Woodhouse received a bachelor of architecture from the University of Illinois at Urbana in 1971. He was an Associate with Stanley Tigerman and Associates from 1975-1979 and Vice President and Senior Associate with Booth/Hansen and Associates from 1980 to 1987.

He has been a visiting critic at the University of Illinois in Chicago and Urbana, and has written articles and book reviews for Progressive Architecture, Inland Architect, A + U, *the* Journal of Architectural Education, *and* Skyline.

Firm: Langdon and Woodhouse

101

Kevin Harrington

The relationship of the container and what is contained has been a topic of importance in architectural theory throughout the modern era. It should come as no surprise, then, that in the interiors that follow commodity and delight derive many of their clues from the firmness of the existing building. Since all the buildings are structural frames, the architects's initial considerations for their interior had to do with reinforcing that order or setting the plan free and adrift against the structure.

Deborah Doyle's New Orleans Night Club, like the broken grid of the Crescent City which wraps itself along the curve of the Mississippi River, is entered along a meander which then splits off into an alluvial plain of eliding and colliding grids, all within the heavy timber of the recycled warehouse in which it is located. As the cranked watercolor shows, the interconnected spaces of the club generate an inviting tension between wondering and knowing where you are. This is done principally by the use of centering devices which are then pulled apart at the perimeter by diagonals and other layering techniques. Much of Chicago's richness has come up the river from New Orleans; Doyle seems to be returning the favor with a club where the Wild Tchapitoulas, Queen Ida Bontemps or Aaron Neville should feel right at home.

Darcy Bonner's set of elements for an apartment in Lake Point Tower presents an ever freer relation to the frame. Yet it would not be a surprise to learn that he spent some time looking at Mies's two tall building projects from the early 1920's, the forms on which George Schipporeit and John Heinrich began their thinking for this building, as well as Mies's other expressions of interiors from that period. Surely the materials parallel: stone of very rich grain, complex metal clips and brackets, glass lit and colored in a variety of ways, intricately turning and opening elements. The particular elements at first seem extraordinarily complex, abstract and sculptural, until one begins to recognize conventions for more prosaic elements. The intricate series of pinioned doors make the kitchen unit reminiscent of a Swiss Army Knife. The relationship of these floating elements to the building suggests the interaction of ripples in a pond as they appear to float in the space which itself seems to float, only lightly tethered to the curving dock of columns. Unlike the drawings of Paolo Portoghesi which describe a very tightly controlled world of concentricity, the almost infinite set of combinations that Bonner's doors and cabinets and walls open and curve into implies a satisfaction in the naturally infinite randomness of nature, as in the differing veins in the marbles.

Gregory Landahl refers to private clubs built between the World Wars as a conceptual source for his designs for the Chicago Bar Association in its new building now under construction and designed by Stanley Tigerman. The two formal dining rooms shown here are very concerned to reinforce the sense of self assurance that derives from knowing exactly where you are. To achieve this sense of order he has overlaid a poche of columnar order on the indistinct frame of the actual building. In order to offset the potential for a static quality for this space, Landahl has varied the rhythm and elevations of the long walls in the gabled room. By using a low horizon line in his drawings, he is also able to show his interest in the ceiling. The resulting gabled and coffered forms should provide a unifying character to the rooms.

Neil Frankel has considered the problem of making three stories of offices for his own firm as one in which visitors see the firm to be dynamic through the diagonal path taken on entry and the swooping verticality of the spiral stair that links all three floors. For the day to day work of the firm a gridded fabric of perimeter offices and grouped draughting tables surround an inner core containing a wide range of support functions. The actual office function moves between two structural frames: one for the elevator core is regular, while the other in the exterior wall has a progressive rhythm that is different on the long and narrow elevations. All three elements use a five foot module.

102

Susan Schneider-Criezis uses a curving path to lead visitors from the elevator lobby to the shared reception area of three related firms. Given the potential confusion of entering such a shared space, she organized the reception area in a very clear, direct and easily ordered manner so that the visitor would feel oriented, welcome and in control. Whereas Frankel faced the problem of making a visitor feel the space to be "designed" but not "far out" thus giving potential clients the view that the firm had special expertise while understanding a client's needs, Schneider-Criezis is principally concerned to ease the apprehension of a visitor to a new place by making the space regular, ordered and understandable. Unlike Landahl's emphasis on the ceiling, she emphasizes the floor as a direct path to the reception desk to reassure the visitor.

The concern for orienting the visitor in commercial interiors is most clearly presented in the Branch Bank designed by William Bauhs. It, too, is symmetrical, axial, ordered and formal. The structural frame is acknowledged by emphasizing the massiveness of the columns, and by extension the solidity of the bank as an institution. Reflecting the current ease designers exhibit when confronted with a powerful frame, Bauhs uses arched opening and round forms here to heighten the sense of volume, strength and solidity whereas an earlier argument would have demanded the repetition of the structural system at all levels of the interior.

This work reflects the completion of a journey through the looking glass of modernist rules. The Furniture Mart, in which Bauhs's bank is located, initially sought to maintain a mural masonry character for this very large building with a necessarily massive frame because of the very high floor loads. Today, a generation or so after the Chicago frame came to be valued for its expressive self, the desire for strength, durability and longevity now includes the insertion of false arches.

103

Interiors

William Bauhs

A national bank offers personal banking in this branch facility. The large existing volume of the space is preserved by keeping all partitions low. Existing columns supporting the upper floors dominate the space and are enhanced by illuminating them with sconces. The resulting illuminated ceiling provides soft general lighting.

The conference room has a lower "roof," to allow the large space to be uninterrupted, while providing acoustic privacy. As the most important room, it is centrally located on axis with the entry and with the structural columns. The receptionist and teller stations are designed as an island in the center of the space. Partial walls provide security and visual screening of the electronic equipment, and open plan offices are positioned on either side of this circulation axis.

104

A partner in Bauhs and Dring Limited, William Bauhs received a bachelor of architecture degree from the University of Illinois at Champaign-Urbana in 1965. He was a project designer with Harry Weese and Associates from 1965 to 1974. In 1974 he received a Francis J. Plym Traveling Fellowship from the University of Illinois at Champaign-Urbana, where he participated in the masters program from 1974 to 1975.

Branch Bank
680 N. Lake Shore Drive, Chicago, Illinois

Contractor: Gerhard F. Meyne Co.
Mechanical & Electrical Engineer: The Austin Company

Darcy R. Bonner, Jr.

The drawings illustrate three elements of the apartment: a bathroom, powder room and wet bar; a kitchen and utility area; and a video equipment cabinet. This last element is made of irregular shapes of sandblasted glass, bolted to a metal frame which supports and encloses the video equipment. The assemblage is then backlit with bright red light. When the doors are opened, a synthetic fog machine is momentarily activated.

Private Apartment
Lake Point Tower, Chicago, Illinois

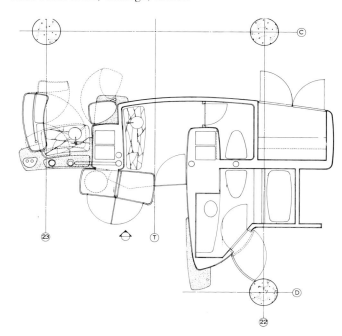

106

A principal at Himmel/Bonner Architects, Darcy Bonner received a bachelor of architecture from Tulane University in 1976 and a master of architecture from the University of Illinois at Chicago in 1981. He worked previously at Booth, Nagle & Hartray, Ltd.

The work he has done with his partner Scott Himmel has received a Distinguished Building Award and an Interior Architecture Award from the Chicago Chapter AIA, an Architectural Woodwork Institute Award, and was a Record Interior of the Year. He has been a guest lecturer at the Architectural League of New York and at the Art Institute of Chicago, where his drawings are in the Burnham Collection. His work has also been exhibited at the Fine Art Gallery of San Diego and Copper Hewitt Museum in New York.

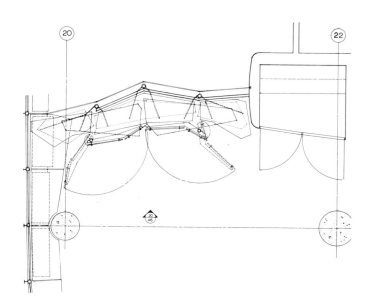

Firm: Himmel/Bonner Architects
Staff: Darcy Bonner with Jim Stapleton and Scott Osterhaus

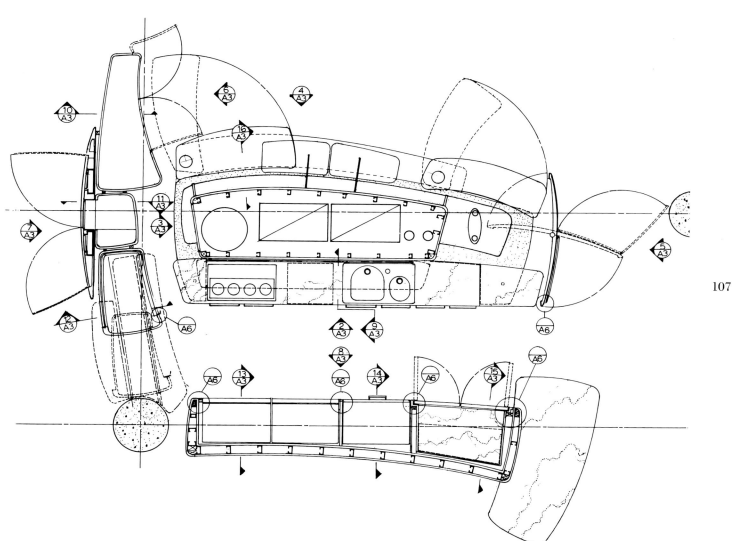

Deborah Doyle

*A principal in Doyle & Ohle Architects, Inc., she received a
bachelor of architecture degree from Illinois Institute of
Technology in 1975 and a graduate diploma from the
Architectural Association of London in 1976. She was an
associate at Stanley Tigerman & Associates, 1976-1980; at
Reichen & Robert in Paris, 1981; and was in private practice
from 1982 to 1987. She is an adjunct assistant professor at the
University of Illinois at Chicago.*

*She was one of the winners of the "Townhouse" competition
sponsored by the Graham Foundation in 1978. Her work has
been in several exhibitions including Late Entries to the Tribune
Tower Competition at the Museum of Contemporary Art in 1980,
and New Chicago Architecture at the Museo di Castelvecchio,
Verona, in 1981. She was editor of volumes 2, 3, and 4 of the
Chicago Architectural Journal.*

City Lights Nightclub
New Orleans, Louisiana

This twelve thousand square foot nightclub is inside an existing
double-height, heavy timber warehouse building in the old
river district. Like nested Russian Easter eggs, there are new
"buildings" placed within this existing building. A resultant
fantasy land of compositionally placed architectural elements
houses the various programmatic components.

As at a formal ball, the attendees follow a curvaceous path
through the anteroom which centers them for introduction at
the formal gateway. From here program is organized to create
the illusion of theater. The user is viewed as a theatrical
participant who elects to be either audience or actor. With the
audience seated in the wings, main players are centerstage on
the dance floor as laser lights play off the overhead trusswork.
The surrounding interior elements work off this center focus as
backdrop scenery.

108

*Firm: Doyle & Ohle Architects, Inc.
Staff: Deborah Doyle, James Ohle, Michael Hartel, Daniella Hanek,
and Mark Lehmann.*

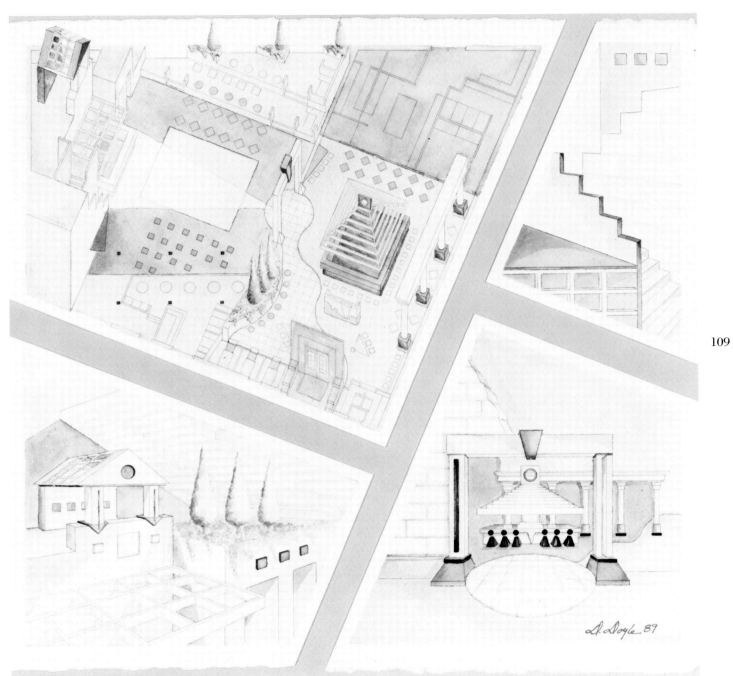

A. Doyle 89

Neil P. Frankel

Perkins and Will's rejuvenated, rapidly growing practice recently gave itself a new working space. Located in the new Wacker Drive building designed by Ralph Johnson of Perkins and Will, it reflects the firm's multi-disciplined approach to design, their philosophy of designing for individual needs, and the vitality characteristic of its recent growth.

The 54,000 sq. ft. space is finished with classical natural materials combined with a contemporary envelope and a neutral color palette. The elevator lobby features the firm's corporate logo outlined in a combination of neon and indirect lighting. Acid-etched white oak floor tiles, stained light gray and accented with dark gray mahogany inlays complete the entry. In the reception area, a freestanding circular staircase provides a focus and vertical circulation. All three floors are visible from the lobby, revealing the firm's vitality and energy.

110

A vice president and design principal of Perkins & Will, he is responsible for interior architecture in their Chicago office. He received a bachelor of architecture degree from the University of Illinois at Urbana in 1960. He is the past chair of the National AIA Committee on Interiors, and was recognized by IBD in 1989 as one of the nation's twenty leading designers. A frequent design critic and juror, in 1988 he juried the Minnesota Society of Architects Interior Architecture Awards and the Hampton Roads Virginia Chapter AIA Distinguished Building Design Awards.

His work has received design awards from the Chicago AIA and National IBD. It has been shown at the Walker Art Center in Minneapolis and it was the subject of the May 1989 cover story of Interiors Magazine.

Perkins & Will Office Interiors
Chicago, Illinois

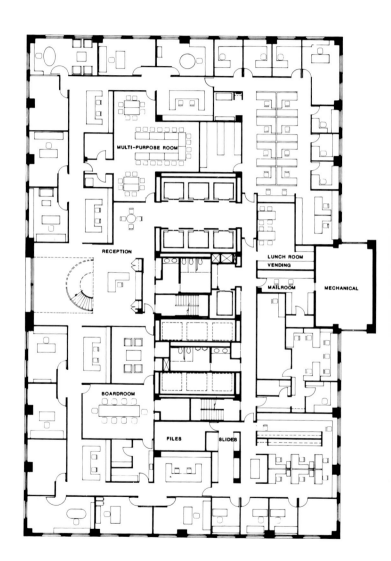

Firm: Perkins & Will
Design: Neil P. Frankel, Davor Engel and Rashne Schroff
Managment: Ken Susinka

111

Gregory W. Landahl

After fifty years on South LaSalle Street, The Chicago Bar Association is building a new headquarters building on South Plymouth Court in the Central Loop. This project is for the interior architecture of the eight floors initially being occupied by The Chicago Bar Association. The program includes a small lobby bar, a fast food dining room, two major dining rooms, three floors of private meeting rooms and multiple floors of administrative offices. A link will be made to the John Marshall Law School.

The concept refers to the great private clubs designed in the period between the First and Second World Wars. The large columns mask inopportune structural columns with poché, and develop other functional areas. Materials and details are handled simply and with an economy of means. The color palette is very soft with strong fabric accents that can be changed with the seasons. Completion is scheduled for mid 1990.

Gregory W. Landahl, AIA, received his degrees in architecture from the University of Illinois at Urbana, after spending a year in the foreign study program at the successor to the French Beaux Arts Academy. He began his career in the Planning and Architecture Studio at Skidmore, Owings & Merrill, developed his interior-architectural philosophy while affiliated with S.O.M. and began to specialize in interior architecture after founding The Landahl Group in 1980. He is the chairman of the Interior Architecture Committee of the Chicago Chapter AIA, and is an officer in the Chicago Interior Design Organization, of which The Landahl Group is a member firm.

Mr. Landahl has taught design at the Art Institute of Chicago and the University of Illinois at Chicago, and has been a guest lecturer and panelist at Art Institute and AIA Conferences. In 1987 he received a Young Architect Award presented by The Chicago Chapter of the AIA.

The Chicago Bar Association Offices
Chicago, Illinois

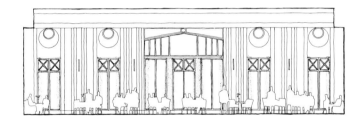

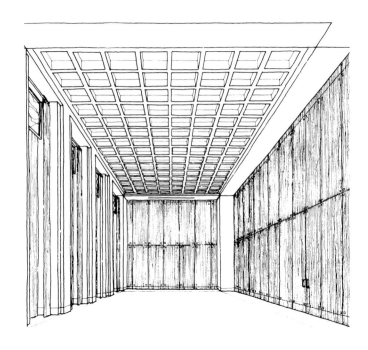

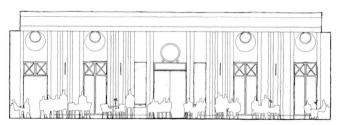

Firm: The Landahl Group, Ltd.
Staff: Greg Landahl, Mark Fischer, and Dan Lanoergan
Project manager: John Kahill

113

Susan Schneider-Criezis

A Principal of Criezis Architects, she received her bachelor of architecture from the University of Notre Dame, and her master of architecture from the Massachusetts Institute of Technology. She has worked for Gelick Foran Associates; Solomon, Cordwell, Buenz & Associates; and Eichstaedt Architects and Planners. From 1980 to 1986 she taught at the University of Illinois in Chicago. She is a member of Chicago Women in Architecture.

Corporate Offices
Evanston, Illinois

The offices of Rynne House Communications, Rynne Marketing Group, and Women's Healthcare Consultants are located on the seventh floor of the 500 Davis Street Building in Evanston. The design centered around a common foyer and conference room for three separate, but related companies. The curves of the foyer draw visitors from the elevator to the entrance of the offices. Raised wood moldings and colored bands link the foyer with work spaces. The entrances to private offices are recessed off of the corridors, which open onto common spaces with natural light.

114

Firm: Criezis Architects

Staff: Susan Schneider-Criezis; Demetrios A. Criezis; Connie Jo Settersten, project architect Interiors: Sandra P. Morrow and Catherine Diamanti

David Van Zanten

As an architect who does not practice, but teaches architectural history instead, I feel intimidated when confronted with these designs. It is no reflection on any of the designs that I shall discuss only a few of them in a more personal and partial response.

There are two things that I greatly value in the experience of visiting a specially-designed home. First is the pleasure of discovering its spatial configuration as I set through the door. This is the most cosmic treat the architect can prepare for the client and the client's guests. Second is the mood created in the dining room, which is the most delicate and important experience in terms of hospitality that the architect can concoct. By reviewing the designs from these two standpoints, I am leaving out such classic points of discussion as style, overall layout, facade composition and detailing. Restricting myself to these two favorite matters, however, permits me in my amateur capacity to be sincere and I hope, interesting.

One sort of entrance immediately permits you to grasp the whole interior space; another permits you a great, if calculated and often deceptive, tableau. In Peter Landon's unpretentious shack the door is at the base of the fan-like configuration so that everything immediately presents itself to you at your first step inside. On the other hand, when you get inside David Haymes's design, it is difficult not to step right out again. There are fourteen doors — all evidently equally possible entrances — leading into only two rooms, so that the interior space lays itself out at once within each one of them. It is a wonderfully easy house; I wish I lived there.

Frederick Phillips's is somewhat the same since the "front door" leads to a deck between two small enclosed house-volumes. Not much happens when you enter either of these volumes, but I suspect a great deal happens when you first step up on the Door County deck. When entering George Pappageorge's cube you are at the bottom of a well, with a glimpse of cylinders and other cubes loosely arranged on levels above you. I would prefer to start from the center of the cube

and to have the option of going up or down, but there is interest in making your visitor climb a bit for his or her architectural dinner.

Richard Whitaker and Roy Solfisburg let you see much of their interiors from the door, but not all, and you can't grasp the inside completely from there.

Stephen Wierzbowski denies us a plan of what one presumes would be an initial tableau as monumental as Margaret McCurry's and Wojciech Madeyski's. McCurry adopts a full-fledged "Beaux Arts" scheme complete with paired facing stairways and double-height hall. I suspect that here the proportions and nuances of volumetric composition would determine success or failure — it is a mighty organ chord and all the notes should harmonize. Madeyski tries to compromise with Modernism. There is a resonance in the elongated, pilastered entrance hall, but I wonder how this will look ending with the spiral staircase in the family room.

In this context, Christopher Rudolph's house puzzles me. Wright also slipped you in the side like this, but only after a good deal of preparation, leading you over terraces and down courts. On the other hand, Wright would give you an axis from the entrance door straight on into a room, sometimes with two minor axes crossing it, but not usually with the disruption of a staircase right at the intersection. It makes me realize how different Wright was from McKim or McCurry, for all his axiality.

In some houses the first step is a non-event, perhaps because of street noise or weather. It might be self evident that the test of an entrance is what you dish up to the visitor just beyond the threshold, but it seems less immediately clear what to serve architecturally in the dining room. This is where the ritual of hospitality is acted out seated and at length, with the meal as the altar furniture and the conversation as the litany. Yet there are as many ways of arranging the service as there are religious sects in our country. Should it be Calvinist and formal with everyone sitting straight and looking inward? Or might it be Catholic with plenty of space behind the seats, windows, porches and everyone coming and going at their pleasure? Or should it be Quaker and minimal so that everyone makes the ritual as it proceeds?

Here Haymes's design excels: the room is square and formal, but big and very open to the outside, so that if you want a breath of fresh air between courses you can be out and back in a trice. Very Quaker. The whole house is really just a dining room.

Madeyski's, Jack Naughton's and Laurence Dieckmann's dining rooms are formal, either three sided enclosures on axis with the living room or, in Naughton's case, shaped in the classic octagon, leaving no space behind the diners for hanky panky or odd furniture. Each has some window or door on one side, but all seem a bit claustrophobic, in a Presbyterian sort of way. McCurry and Solfisburg, in spite of the axiality of their schemes, have you set off to one side of the living room — a venerated tradition of the Adirondack camp which breaks down formality. But here in Chicago it would lack the sound of loons filtering in through the windows. Very few of these dining rooms would permit one to place a desk in a corner, and none consciously provide for it.

In some of the designs dining becomes spatially quite informal: you find the space you like, then eat in it. This seems true of Pappageorge and Landon. In Frederick Wilson's design tables are indicated in the plans, but to my mind the spaces around them do not suggest their location. I could imagine the owners shoving the tables around a good deal as time passes. However, Phillips's dining room strikes a fine balance between formality and ease, carrying on the axis of the living room but up several steps and given the view. It appears that we design better vacation houses than city dwellings, or at least their associations are more comforting.

Single Family Residences

Stuart Cohen

This addition to a stone and slate roofed house extends the vocabulary with subtle variations. The 1930's house, which equivocates between French Norman and English Tudor, is given a push by the addition of a half-timber hall used as a family room.

A principal in Stuart Cohen & Associates, Mr. Cohen received his bachelor of architecture and master of architecture degrees from Cornell University. From 1981 to 1988 he practiced in partnership with Anders Nereim. He is an Associate Professor at the University of Illinois at Chicago, and has been a visiting critic and lecturer at universities throughout the country.

His work has been included in numerous exhibits including the Venice Biennale in 1980 and Revision of the Modern, which toured Europe. His designs have received Distinguished Building awards from the Chicago Chapter AIA, and awards from Progressive Architecture *magazine.*

Highland Park House Addition
Highland Park, Illinois

Architects: Stuart Cohen & Associates
Project Architect: Julie Hacker
Project Team: Stuart Cohen, Julie Hacker, and Eric Ward.

Laurence E. Dieckmann

The house sits on a wooded dune and has a progression of experiences, from the approach through the woods, up through the rusticated entry of the house, to the semi-circular solarium opposite the entry. The house is organized along an axis running from front to back, but the path is never exactly centered until one enters the living area and solarium, where a strong cross axis is established. The solarium projects into the trees at the crest of the dune, and has the feel of a tree house. The living and dining areas are elevated to take advantage of views into the woods and across the dunes, and the bedrooms below open into intimate private glades behind the entry wall. The plan and elevation are in tension between the ideas of axial arrangement and casual adjustment to particular conditions, and thus between formal composition and vernacular reference.

120

Currently with Roula Associates, Laurence Dieckmann received a master of architecture in 1970 from Washington University. He has been an instructor in the Energy in Architecture course offered at AIA Midwest and Regional conferences, and has taught at the University of Illinois in Chicago.

He won a Progressive Architecture *Design Citation in 1982, and is the co-author of the* Hawkweed Passive Solar House Book. *His work has been published in* Inland Architect *and* Solar Age *Magazines, and has been exhibited at the Art Institute of Chicago.*

Boelter Residence
Beverly Shores, Indiana

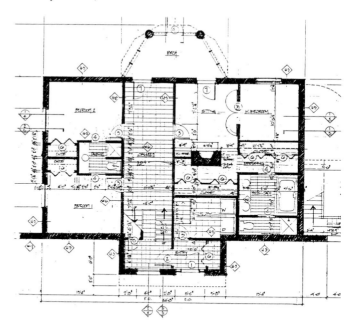

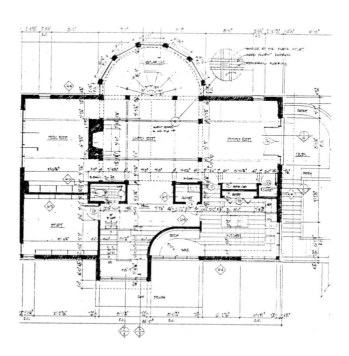

Firm: L.E. Dieckmann, Architect

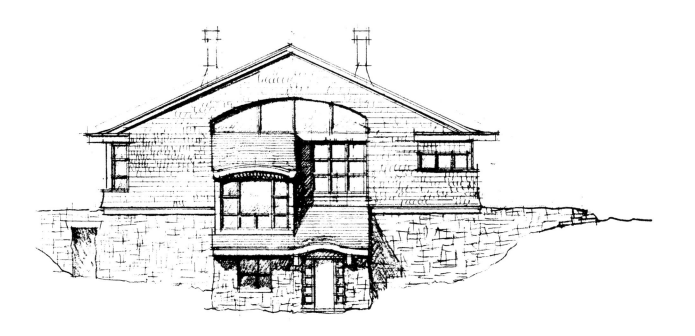

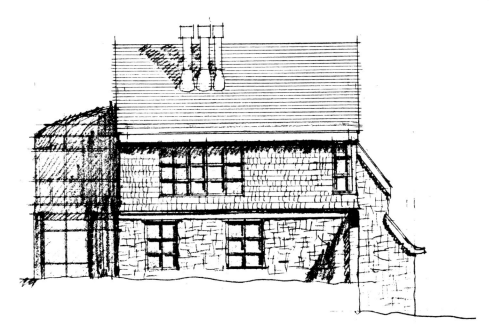

Garret Eakin

This speculative house recalls the typology of Chicago's Victorian "greystones" in materials and texture. The facade is layered with smooth-cut and split-face limestone, which allows a duality of scales and energizes the principal elevations with light, shadow and texture. Lintels are not expressed, in order to allow this variety in scale. The tripartite plan has three shapes: a square, a circle and a rectangle, connected by bridges. The square volume contains a colonaded entry with library above, overlooking the two story living room. Above this volume is located a guest suite with an open breezeway. The square portion of the plan is connected to the private family quarters via the cylindrical stair. This zone of the house opens up to the quiet rear decks and elevated views of the master bedroom terrace. The overall concept recalls the "greystone" precedent with a new sense of sculpted variety and surprise.

122

A partner in Banks/Eakin, Architects since 1979, he received degrees from Oklahoma State University in 1971 and from the University of Illinois at Urbana in 1973. He worked for Skidmore, Owings & Merrill in 1973 and for Perkins & Will from 1974 to 1978. His work has received a Distinguished Interior Architecture Award from the Chicago Chapter AIA, an Award for Interior Design from Restaurant and Institution, *and First Place in the interior design competitions held in 1981 and 1982 by* Interior Design Magazine.

He is an Associate Professor at the School of the Art Institute of Chicago, where his drawings are in the permanent collection. He is a member of the Landmarks Preservation Council in Illinois, the Frank Lloyd Wright Home and Studio Foundation, and the Urban Space Committee of the Friends of Downtown. He is currently completing a book on interior architecture with John Kurtich, which is funded by a grant from the Graham Foundation.

1942 North Orchard
Chicago, Illinois

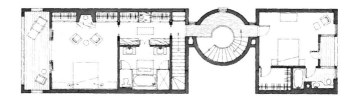

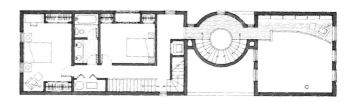

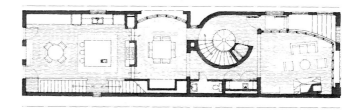

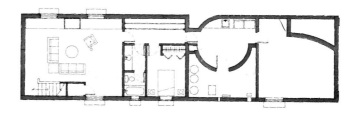

Firm: Banks/Eakin Architects
Client: J.S. Drew Construction
Staff: Garret Eakin, John Banks, Mike Venechuk, George Krassas.

David A. Haymes

Planned as a year-round second home, the Melto Residence is located on a small wedge-shaped lot near southern Lake Michigan. With its long sides facing north and south, the 18′ x 70′ plan allows all spaces to take advantage of views as well as summer breezes. Inside, the house is an informal succession of spaces linked by a perimeter of French doors and blue stone flooring. The living area fills a two and a half story volume, interrupted by a truss bridge that connects sleeping areas above. The exterior materials of champagne colored plaster, white trim, and cedar shutters, soon to age gray, combine to evoke a comfortable villa imagery.

124

A principal with Pappageorge/Haymes, Ltd., he received his bachelor of architecture degree from the University of Illinois at Chicago in 1978. He was a James Scholar and received a citation of Excellence for his design thesis. Prior to forming a partnership with George Pappageorge in 1981, he worked for Kenneth A. Schroeder Associates and HSW in Chicago. He has taught at the University of Illinois.

His work has received numerous AIA Distinguished Building awards, and has been published in Progressive Architecture, Interiors, Architecture, *and* Inland Architect, *among other journals.*

Melto Residence
Timberlane Estates, Michigan

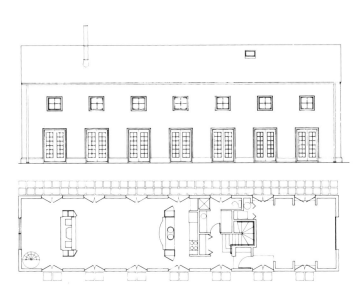

Firm: Pappageorge/Haymes, Ltd.
Staff: David Haymes with George Pappageorge

Karen Johnson

A partner in Johnson, Rogatz, and Wilson, Karen Johnson is an architect with a degree in design from the University of Cincinnati and a master of architecture degree from the University of Illinois at Chicago. She was previously the president of Karen Johnson Associates, Inc., an interior design firm, and a project architect with Hammond Beeby and Babka, Tilton & Lewis Associates, and Skidmore, Owings & Merrill. She has also taught at the University of Wisconsin in Milwaukee.

She has been responsible for several award-winning and published projects, and her work has been exhibited at The Chicago Historical Society and in the "Divine Detail Show."

The Smolin Residence
DePaul, Illinois

The project is a new two story concrete block and limestone house on a vacant lot on the near north side of Chicago. The clients, a couple in their early 30's, requested an oval dining room, curves throughout the house, and extra space planned for a future family. The curvilinear glass block panels penetrate the exterior facade, and reveal the interior forms of the house. An office/party room is also planned for the third floor.

126

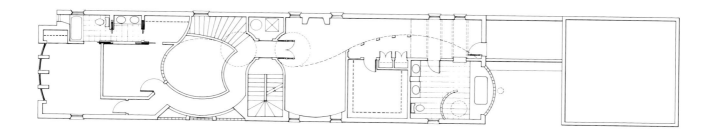

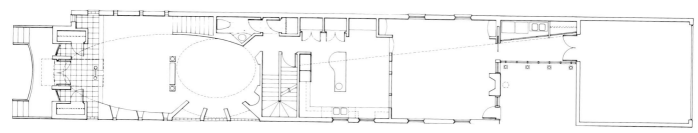

Firm: Johnson, Rogatz, and Wilson
Staff: Karen Johnson with Frederick Wilson, Frederick Harboe, and Jon Splitt

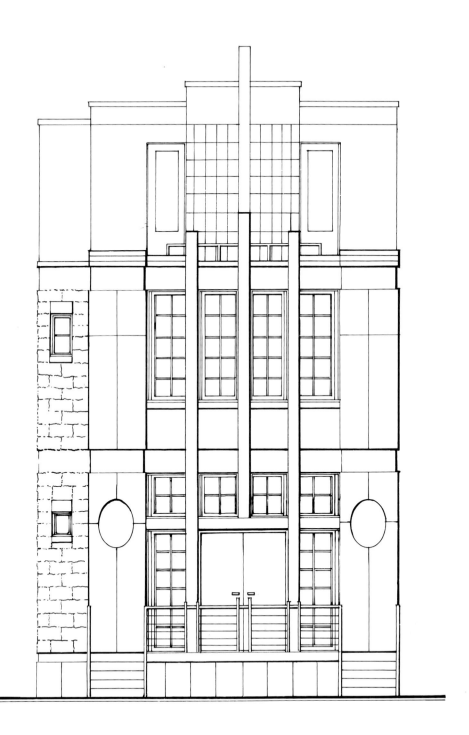

Peter Landon

Minimalism characterizes this project in terms of space, material construction, and cost. Beginning with a simple two-story box, the walls and roof were gently angled to fit the requirements of the interior. The garage space was reduced to the smallest possible volume, which determined the angled edge of the work space and the floor of the loft above. Where the corner tapers off of the volume, the angled stair becomes a dynamic aspect of the space. The interior materials are a minimalist plywood finished floor and exposed roof deck, drywall walls, and no window, door, or base trim. The exterior was finished with redwood plywood panels set in a grid of galvanized metal beads, and corrugated fiberglass awnings on wood brackets over the entryways. With function, simplicity, and cost as the project's essential concerns, the challenge was to explore ways to express these concerns, without sacrificing the formal aspects of the design.

128

Born in Chicago in 1949, Peter Landon graduated from Kansas University in 1971, and for the next three years worked with a design/build team of architects on various projects across the country. He worked with Paolo Soleri, Harry Weese, and for ten years with Weese Hickey Weese Architects until early 1987 when he formed his own practice: Peter Landon Architects Ltd.

Peter was a co-founder of the Architects Forum, visiting critic at University of Illinois at Chicago, and guest lecturer at various organizations in and around the city. He has been on the Mayor's Neighborhood Task Force, treasurer of the Chicago Architectural Club and was chairman of the Chicago Chapter AIA Design Committee for four years. His work has been exhibited at various locations and published in Architectural Record, Progressive Architecture, Inland Architect *and* Home Magazine. *He won a best of show citation in 1983 for New Voices/New Visions and won a CCAIA Young Architect Award in 1986.*

Martin/Savage Studio
Oak Park, Illinois

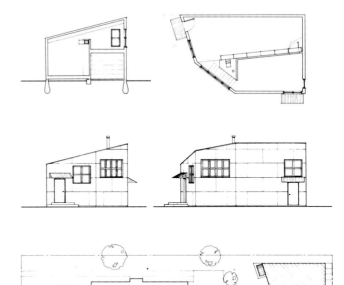

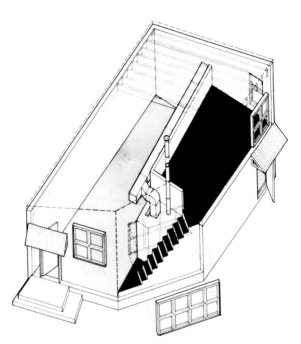

Firm: Peter Landon Architects, Ltd.
Staff: Peter Landon with Craig Bass

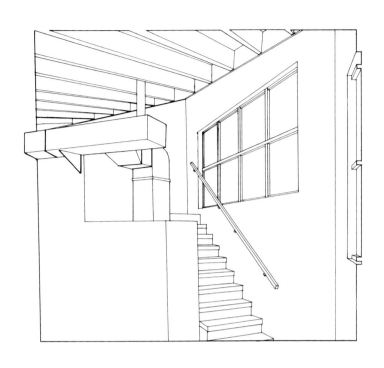

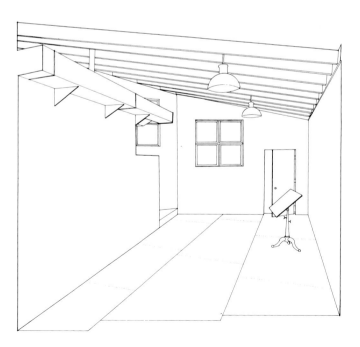

Wojciech Madeyski

This 4000 sq. ft. house is located on a heavily wooded site, and it encloses 5 bedrooms within a compact two story shell. The plan of the house is organized along the east/west axis of the site. A variety of skylit spaces, differently articulated in terms of height and volume, form the skeleton of the house. The majority of the functional areas are accessible off this private mini-mall, with a varying degree of privacy. Daily activities benefit from sunny exposures, while most spaces have multiple views toward the surroundings. Construction of concrete masonry features a variety of textures and colors, integrated into an elaborate decorative design.

130

A principal in Voy Madeyski Architects Ltd., he was formerly a senior vice president and design principal with Perkins & Will. He received his master of architecture from the University of Warsaw in 1962. He worked in Paris from 1963 to 1966, with Fitch and Laroca from 1966 to 1968, and C.F. Murphy Associates from 1968 to 1976.

His projects have received Distinguished Building Awards from the Chicago Chapter AIA, and have been exhibited at the Art Institute of Chicago, the Museum of Science and Industry, and in museums and art galleries in Chicago and in Europe. He is also a painter and a visiting professor of design at the University of Illinois at Urbana.

Buch Residence
Gurnee, Illinois

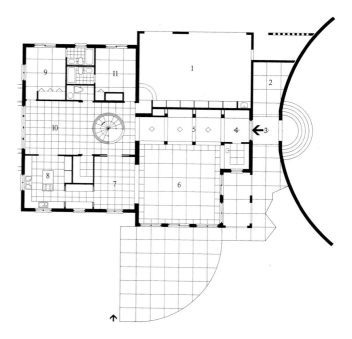

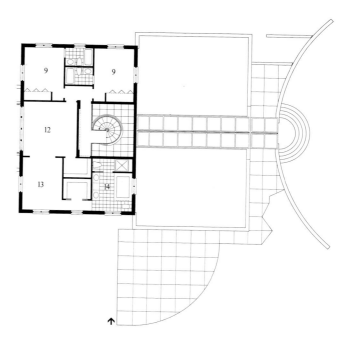

Firm: Voy Madeyski Architects Ltd.

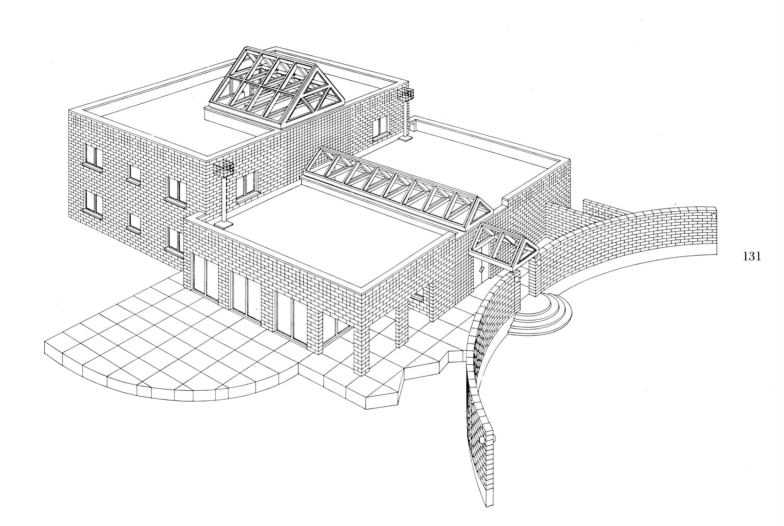

William Alan McBride

The Lackner House in Kenilworth was designed in 1904 by George W. Maher. Its highly original design shows various stylistic influences, particularly the Austrian Seccessionist Movement. While the house has been restored by the owners, their modern use patterns required the addition of a family room, the improvement of the "family entrance," and the replacement of an insensitively designed screened porch. The materials and massing of the addition respect Maher's design intent while defining spaces for contemporary living.

132

A principal in the firm of McBride and Kelley Architects, Ltd., he received a master of architecture degree from the Harvard Graduate School of Design in 1976. He has worked for Harry Weese and Associates and John Portman and Associates. He received a Frederick Sheldon Traveling Fellowship from Harvard University in 1976.

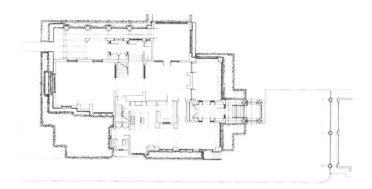

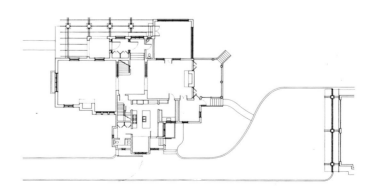

Firm: McBride and Kelley
Architects Staff: Richard Merrifield, Mary Walters and Kathy Hrabovsky

Margaret McCurry

Sited on a slope near a small lake in the Kettle Moraine region along the Illinois-Wisconsin border, this country home establishes linkages with a diverse collection of American ancestors, while remaining a unique product of the melding of Western and Eastern cultures. Designed as a diminutive estate for a Japanese couple who commute regularly between Chicago and Tokyo, the property includes a tennis court and pavilion which form an east-west axis with trellised guest parking and garages. A spruce-lined allée leads to the main house, which is in the American vernacular tradition, but also possesses a spatial order and dignity that responds to its Japanese owners. The house is bisected from north to south by a nine-foot-wide two-story space, and then reconnected by a bridge between the two second-story wings. The image is a village street with upper stories overhanging and overlooking the passageways below. An east-west cross-axis flows under the bridge, linking the outer single-story wings. Axial vistas extend through the house and into the landscape, establishing the symmetry and order so prized by client and architect alike.

134

A partner in Tigerman McCurry, she received a bachelor of arts degree from Vassar College in 1964. She worked for Skidmore, Owings & Merrill from 1966 to 1977 and was in private practice from 1977 to 1982. She has been chairperson of long range planning for the Committee on Design of the National AIA, and was a vice president of the Chicago Chapter. She has served on design juries for the AIA, NEA, PA, and IBD, received a Loeb Fellowship from Harvard University in 1986-87, and has taught at the School of the Art Institute of Chicago.

Her work has received an Honor Award from the National AIA; Distinguished Building Awards and Interior Architecture Awards from the Chicago Chapter AIA, a "Big I" award from Interiors *magazine, a grand prize from* Builder *magazine for House of the Year, and has been exhibited at the Art Institute of Chicago and the Chicago Historical Society.*

Private Residence
Fox Lake, Illinois

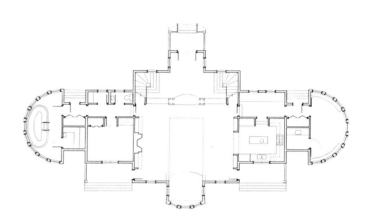

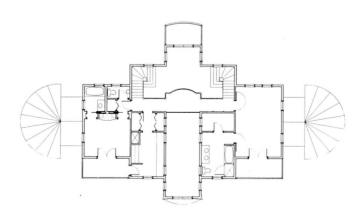

Firm: Tigerman McCurry
Staff: Margaret McCurry with Roger N. Farris, project architect

NORTH ELEVATION
1/4" = 1'- 0"

SOUTH ELEVATION
1/4" = 1'- 0"

Jack Naughton

This project is driven by an overt application of geometry in plan. It is being used to make and interrelate a series of rooms perceived as separate and contained.

The subject of study is the implication of rigid axial plan relationships on the "casual" appearance of the house. Consequently, the plans and elevations as shown represent negotiations in process.

Project for a Private Residence
Northeast Ohio

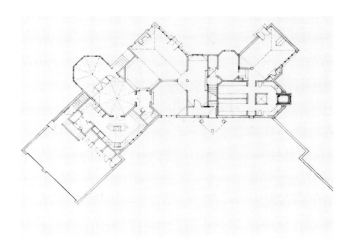

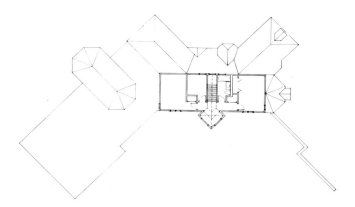

136

Jack Naughton holds two professional degrees in architecture, both from the University of Illinois at Chicago where he is presently teaching. After relationships with several firms in the Chicago area, he entered private practice in 1983. He has taught at the Institute for Architecture and Urban Studies, Yale University, the University of Illinois at Urbana, and he is a Fellow of the American Academy in Rome.

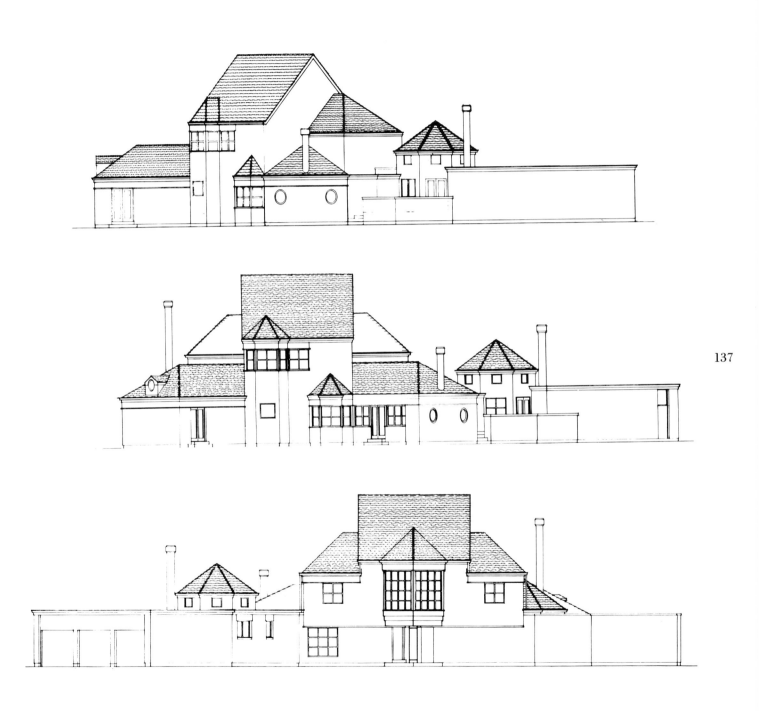

George C. Pappageorge

A principal with Pappageorge/Haymes, Ltd., George Pappageorge received his bachelor of architecture degree from the University of Illinois at Chicago in 1978, having attended their overseas study program at the Ecole des Beaux-Arts in Versailles from 1974 to 1975. Prior to forming a partnership with David Haymes in 1981, he worked for Kenneth A. Schroeder Associates, Rudich Pappageorge Architect, and Urban Planning Consultants, all in Chicago.

His work has received Interior Awards and Distinguished Building awards from the Chicago Chapter of the AIA, and has been published in Progressive Architecture, Interiors, Architecture, *and* Inland Architect, *among other journals. He is a member of the AIA, and has taught at the University of Illinois at Urbana.*

Nemickas Residence

Taking advantage of views at the southern tip of Lake Michigan, this 3,500 square foot vacation residence reflects the client's desire for a modernist treehouse for grownups. The main volume of the home is a thirty-six foot cube inserted into a hillside next to the progressively larger planes of the parking area and exterior deck. Within this simple geometry, rectilinear masses are playfully arranged, one per floor, to house internally focused functions. Anchored only by a cylindrical stair, the sleeping level rotates out of the main volume. While appearing to float, it defines the formal functions of the first floor and more private areas of the loft.

Firm: Pappageorge / Haymes, Ltd.

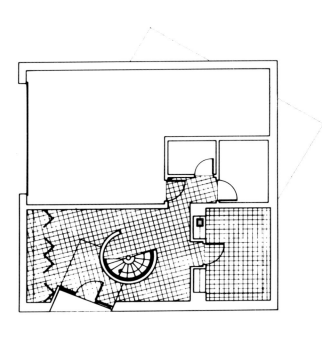

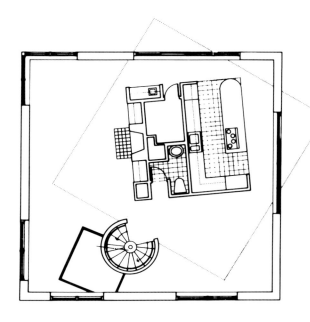

139

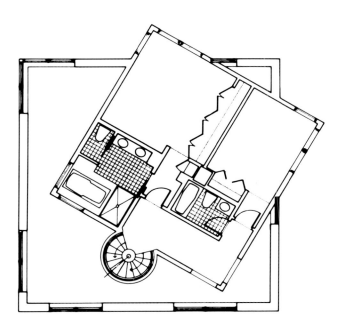

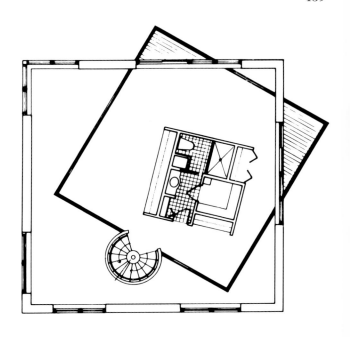

Frederick Phillips

This 1300 square foot summer residence is inspired by the rural farms of Wisconsin. The program is organized into three distinct structures; for living, sleeping, and bathing respectively.

140

A principal in the firm of Frederick Phillips & Associates, he received a bachelor of arts from Lake Forest College in 1969 and a master of architecture from the University of Pennsylvania in 1973. From 1974 to 1975 he worked for Harry Weese and Associates. He has taught and been a visiting critic at the University of Illinois at Chicago, and he has lectured at Notre Dame University, the Merchandise Mart, the Chicago Architecture Foundation, City House, and the Lake Forest Preservation Foundation.

His firm has received Distinguished Building Awards from the Chicago Chapter AIA and a Gold Medal from the Illinois / Indiana Masonry Council. It has been exhibited at the Art Institute of Chicago, and published in Architectural Record, Progressive Architecture, Architecture, *and* Inland Architect *magazines.*

Private Residence
Washington Island, Door County, Wisconsin

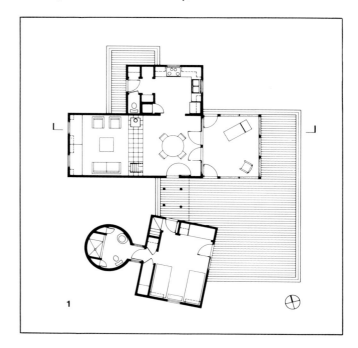

1

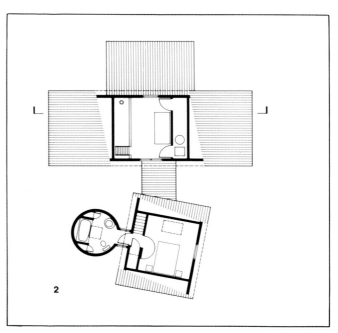

2

Firm: Frederick Phillips & Associates

NORTH

EAST

SOUTH

WEST

SECTION

WEST

141

NORTH

EAST

SOUTH

Kathryn Quinn

A partner in Quinn and Searl, Architects, she received a bachelor of architecture degree from the University of Illinois at Chicago in 1977. She was an associate with Hammond, Beeby and Babka Architects, and has worked at Harry Weese and Associates and with Stuart Cohen. She is treasurer of the Chicago Architectural Club (1988-1990).

Her work has been included in several exhibitions, including the National AIA Women in Architecture show, the Klein Gallery, the Chicago Historical Society and the Archicenter. Both Interior Design *and* Inland Architect *magazines have recently featured her work.*

A Stair for a Lincoln Park Residence
Chicago, Illinois

All of the formal spaces on the first floor of this townhouse are oriented to the 25 foot side yard. The cherry-lined entry hall, with a built-in armoire at each end, leads through a vaulted space to the main stairhall. The cherry paneling continues into the stairhall, inlaid with bronze strips and bronze sections at each end. The raised cherry frame becomes a vertical screen and balustrade for the staircase. The bronze detailing then develops into a decorative frieze around the stairwell opening, completing the motif.

142

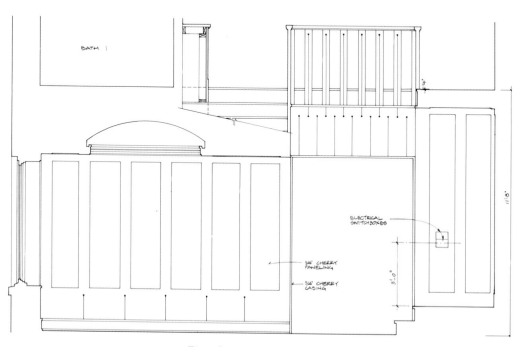

Firm: Quinn and Searl, Architects
Staff: Kathryn Quinn, Linda Searl, and Debra McQueen
Model: Lorenzo Esquival

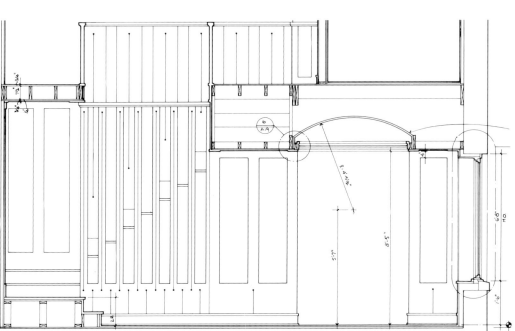

Christopher H. Rudolph

Principal of Rudolph & Associates P.C., he received a bachelor of architecture from the Illinois Institute of Technology in 1975. He has taught at Columbia College, the University of Illinois at Chicago, and the School of the Art Institute, and currently teaches at Illinois Institute of Technology. He founded the Chicago Architectural Press Incorporated, and as president of Exedra Books he republished the Schinkel Sammlung in 1981. He has lectured widely and is currently a director of the Unity Temple Restoration Foundation.

In 1985, he received a Young Architect Award from the Chicago Chapter AIA, and in 1986 he was selected as one of "Forty Under Forty" by the Architectural League of New York and Interiors *magazine. He was a finalist in the Oak Park Studio Row Competition, and the Chicago Bar Association's Young Architects Exhibition. His work has been exhibited at the Art Institute of Chicago, the Museum of Science and Industry, the Merchandise Mart, the ArchiCenter, Morton and Barat colleges, and IIT. It is in the Burnham Library Collection and has been published in* Inland Architect, Threshold, Architectural Digest, *and* Chicago Magazine.

144

Häus Madison

This house is a special refuge hidden in the landscape, set among the trees. Its mass is preceded by horizontal layers that establish a natural plateau. The verticals are indigenous masonry piers, implying eroded stone outcrops which project through terra firma. The chambers of the house radiate from the core, stretching and projecting in every direction. As an organic product, romantic and picturesque, the architecture reconstitutes a layered paradise from within the landscape.

Firm: Rudolph and Associates, P.C.
Acknowledgements: F. L. Wright, T. H. Beeby, and S. K. Robinson

Kenneth A. Schroeder

This house consists of four distinct volumes hinged around a main drum. The main cylinder is detached from the ground providing an entrance to the structure and a central carport. The exposed structural columns rise through the building, organizing the interior spaces. The interior becomes an assembly of living areas shaped according to their particular functions. Cuts into the cylinder made possible three degrees of enclosure within it: interior rooms, screened-in porch, and an open deck.

One extension from the cylinder provides an entrance stairway into the residence and a complete guest wing. Another volume contains a garage with a rooftop whirlpool and an in-ground swimming pool beside it. Both can be reached from a bridge connecting the garage to the main house porch. The exterior finishes include vertical cedar and corrugated metal siding.

146

Kenneth A. Schroeder is the founding principal of the firm Schroeder Murchie Laya Associates, Ltd. He is a graduate of the University of Illinois and received his master of architecture from the University of Toronto in 1971. An AIA and NCARB member, Mr. Schroeder is currently an Associate Professor at the University of Illinois at Chicago.

Before founding his own firm in 1976, Mr. Schroeder participated as a design partner in the firm Hinds, Schroeder and Whitaker. His work has been recognized in numerous national and international publications and he has received several design awards.

The Private Residence of Mort & Coots Siegel
Michiana, Michigan

Firm: Schroeder Murchie Laya Associates, Ltd.
Staff: Kenneth A. Schroeder, Jack Murchie, Jack Stoneberg

Perspective Drawings: Jack Murchie
Model, Painting, Line Drawing: Jack Stoneberg

Linda Searl

*A partner of Quinn and Searl, Architects, she received a
bachelor of architecture 1971, and a master of architecture in
1973, both from the University of Florida. Prior to founding
Quinn and Searl, Architects in 1985, she worked for Nagle,
Hartray and Associates. She has taught at the University of
North Carolina at Charlotte, Florida A & M University, the
University of Illinois at Chicago, and the University of
Wisconsin at Milwaukee. She is a Director of the Chicago
Chapter AIA, and chairs their Design Committee and the
Publications Committee.*

*Her work was included in the National AIA Women in
Architecture show, and the Chicago Chapter AIA's Divine Details
show, and was exhibited at the Klein Gallery. She was a finalist
in the Oak Park Studio Row Competition.*

Lincoln Park Townhouse Remodeling and Addition
Chicago, Illinois

The existing Queen Anne townhouse takes up a double city lot.
In remodeling the 9,000 sq. ft. house with an addition, we re-
oriented the plan toward the adjacent lot to the south. The
original part of the house has a cranked corner bay which turns
the corner to the flat side elevation, which has a 30 degree bay.
Our addition responds by joining the addition to the existing
house with a curved two-story copper-clad bay. The rest of the
new side facade has simple arched masonry openings which
match the original's accented brick arches and corbeled
parapet. The first floor steps down into the rear family room
and kitchen with an articulated section and ceiling plan, which
also makes a more direct connection to the garden.

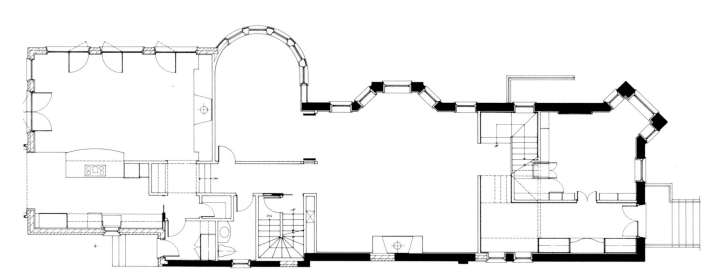

Firm: Quinn and Searl, Architects
Staff: Linda Searl, Kathryn Quinn, Debra McQueen

Roy J. Solfisburg

This vacation house was designed to be set off against wild tropical vegetation. Its sculptural quality is intensified by its reflection in the adjacent lake. By code, all houses on Sanibel must be built twelve feet above mean tide. This put the main living level on the second floor, so that it would not be damaged by water during a hurricane. The ground level space is thus left for a garage. The front elevation is a plane with a strong three-story impact, which makes this small house seem large. A dense grid of curtain-wall and lattice is punctured by a second story recess. The symmetrically sloping eaves of the two roof-lines unify the house into a strong sculptural object.

150

A design partner at Holabird & Root, he received his undergraduate degree from Williams College and his graduate degree from the University of Pennsylvania. In twenty years of practice, he has contributed to the profession through service in the national and local AIA, the Chicago Architectural Assistance Center, and local historic preservation groups. His designs have won national and local awards and are published regularly in the national architectural press and local newspapers.

Casa Chameleon
Sanibel Island, Florida

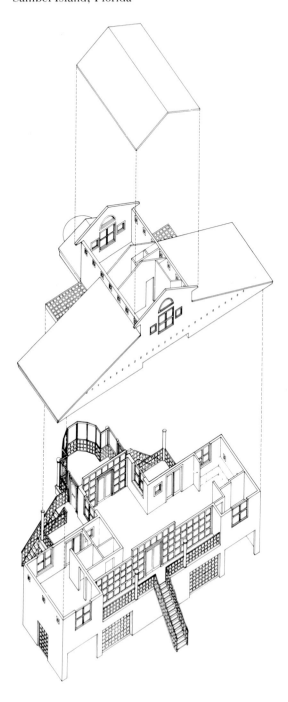

Architects: Roy J. Solfisburg and Max I. Yellin

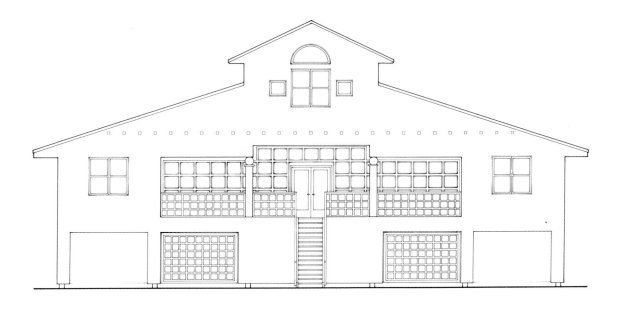

Richard R. Whitaker

This house on Sanibel Island, off Florida's West coast, embraces the spirit of the place while responding to the client's specific requirements. Raised up to catch the breezes and views, and to avoid high water, the house provides open spaces coupled with secluded ones, each with its special character and views. The house is a square pavilion raised on piers in the tradition of an island vernacular generated by climate, materials, and lifestyle. It is entered by a broad stair leading through a series of pierced openings to a central aedicule, which is the physical and psychological center of the house. Capped with a simple hip roof and clerestory over the central space, its edges are notched out to accommodate decks, let in light, and accentuate the individual spaces and the continually changing quality of the light, weather, and views. It is a house where there are many places for the "lion," or perhaps more appropriate, the "alligator" to hide.

152

A design consultant to Riverside Architects and HSW, Ltd., Mr. Whitaker graduated from the University of California at Berkeley in 1961. He was a partner in Moore, Lyndon, Turnbull, and Whitaker, and was the Director of Education for the National AIA. He has taught at the University of California, Berkeley; the University of Colorado, the University of Wisconsin. He is currently a Professor of Architecture and Dean of the College of Architecture, Art and Urban Planning at the University of Illinois at Chicago. In 1982 he served as president of the Chicago Architecture Club.

He has lectured and been a visiting critic at several schools, and has participated in a wide variety of national design award and competition juries. His architectural design work has received numerous national and local AIA awards, an award for environmental excellence from the State of California, and has been published extensively in the national and international press.

Sanibel Island House
Sanibel, Florida

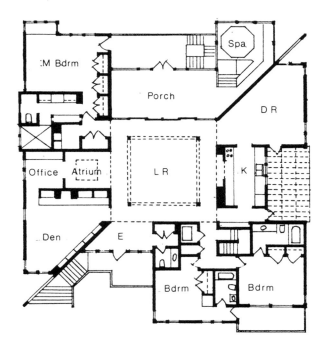

Firm: Riverside Architects

Stephen Wierzbowski

Meers Residence

The design for this house in Lake Forest is a hybrid of aspects of several preliminary studies. The north entry elevation is low and massive: a central block is flanked by service and swimming pool wings. The south garden elevation is tall and open: a variation of the Edwardian classical style. Approaching the house, a diagonal vista of the entry court opens to the southwest. The court is defined by the house and clipped trees, and the landscaping will include a prairie garden, an orchard and a walled rose garden.

154

A principal in the firm of Florian-Wierzbowski, Stephen Wierzbowski received a bachelor of architecture from Carnegie-Mellon University in 1975 and a master of architecture from the University of Illinois at Chicago in 1982. He worked for Machado/Silvetti in 1975 and for Skidmore, Owings & Merrill as a project designer and computer programmer from 1975 to 1981. He has taught at Carnegie-Mellon, and at the University of Illinois in Chicago and in Versailles. He has been a visiting juror at Yale and at the University of Wisconsin at Milwaukee. He curated the exhibit "The Idea of BIG" at Gallery 400, the University of Illinois at Chicago in 1985.

His buildings and exhibit designs have won several awards from the Chicago Chapter of the AIA, the "1986 Retail Design of the Year" from Interiors *magazine, and two awards from* Industrial Design *magazine in 1987. His work has been exhibited in Chicago, London, and Paris, and has been published in* Architectural Digest, Town and Country, Progressive Architecture, Interiors Magazine, The New York Times, *and* Vogue Decoration.

Firm: Florian-Wierzbowski Architecture, P.C.
Staff: Paul Florian, Stephen Wierzbowski, William Worn, Susan Morrow and Jeffrey S. Henriksen

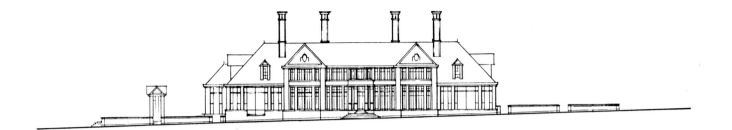

Drawings: Stephen Wierzbowski

Frederick Wilson

Located on a double lot on the near north side of Chicago, the house takes advantage of the views of the city to the south east by stepping back in plan. Designed as a three-flat, the house is planned for future use as a single family house with income units on the first two floors. The main living spaces begin on the third floor taking advantage of views to the city and the garden below. The building steps back in elevation to reduce its vertical scale.

156

A principal of Johnson, Rogatz, Wilson, Architects, Mr. Wilson received his bachelor of architecture from the Ohio State University and his master of architecture from the University of Illinois at Chicago. Mr. Wilson was previously an Associate of Tigerman, Fugman, McCurry, and he has taught at the University of Illinois at Chicago. He has designed several award-winning residential, commercial, and interior design projects, and his work was in the Chicago Chapter AIA's "Divine Details" show.

Private Residence
Chicago, Illinois

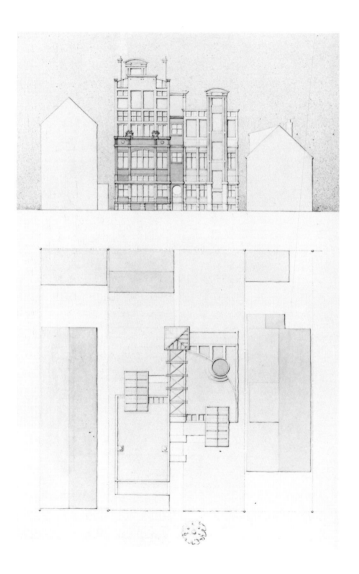

Firm: Johnson, Rogatz, and Wilson
Staff: Fred Wilson with Karen Johnson, Patricia A. Craig, Anne Cunningham, Tom Jacobs, and Jon Splitt

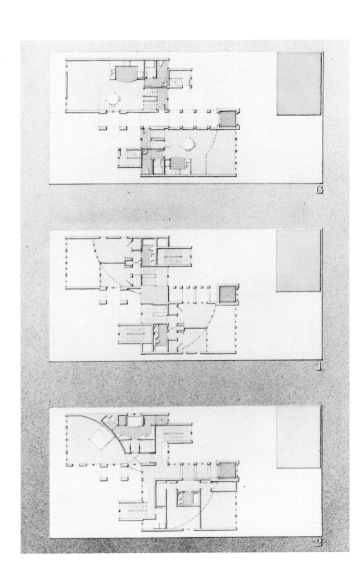

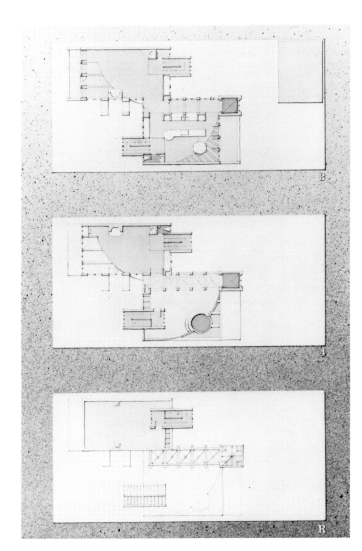

157

Wim de Wit

This year the category of multi-family housing is a varied one. Strictly speaking, only two of the six projects presented here belong in this category. It may be significant that of these two only one design — the one by Swan — is for a Chicago neighborhood; the other — by Tigerman — is for a city in Japan. A third project — by Nereim — is a two-family vacation home, which is presumably only used on week-ends and for holidays.

The other projects in the multi-family housing group are more institutional in character. They range from special facilities for children with emotional and behavioral disorders, to a house for victims of family violence, to a housing complex for senior citizens. Does this paucity of multi-family projects by Club members reflects a general tendency among architects in Chicago? Have we had our fill of the townhouse complexes which abound in Old Town and other yuppie areas, which were so well represented in previous volumes of this Journal? And if we have reached a limit, is it because developers no longer consider them to be profitable? Or are architects simply getting so bored with townhouses that they aren't eager to present them here, as examples of their latest work? The answer is probably all of the above. Whatever the case, if the work of the Architectural Club members presents a cross section of what is happening in Chicago architecture, we should be worried about what we do not see here, for there remains a need for well designed apartment complexes for all levels of society.

Of the two projects that strictly qualify as multi-family housing, only David Swan's Kennicott Place, in Chicago's Kenwood neighborhood is one of those townhouse complexes mentioned above. He has created an elegant street space with two facing rows of houses, which appear to be inspired by the "cottage-vernacular" architecture of Chicago's south side. Mr. Swan's project makes use of important elements such as porches, outside stairs and bays which allow for an extension of a family's private life onto the street. As a dead-end street, Kennicott Place seems to be particularly appropriate for this kind of street life.

Stanley Tigerman's mixed-use apartment building in Fukuoka City Japan, seems at first glance like a stack of small, shifting cubicles. In fact, it is a 6-story building with 3 apartments per floor grouped around an inner court. The building has a square plan, but its regularity is interrupted on the northwest side where a corner is missing. The absence of that corner is emphasized by grid-like screens, which cut through the apartments and seem to hold together the bays and balconies. In the northwest corner, these screens stand totally free in space, emphasizing the gaping hole they simultaneously mask.

Anders Nereim's design for two vacation condominiums in a small barn is an exercise in the use of space. He has managed to slide three levels into the little structure, while dividing it up into two equal and interlocking condominiums. Nereim's vocabulary shows clearly that the design is made in the late 1980's, but in spirit the house is related to the Schroeder house of 1924 by the Dutch architect Gerrit Rietveld. In particular, the organization of the small space and the way in which this space can be opened up by sliding doors makes the vacation home a contemporary "Minimum Existenz" study.

The institutional projects in the multi-family housing series all bear witness to the premise that health and social organizations want their structures to look like residences. Yet, these designs are remarkably varied in the ways they arrange the functions needed by such institutions: rooms for patients or clients, offices, kitchens, dining rooms, meeting rooms, etc.

Diane Legge's Master Plan for a Residential Treatment Facility for Children shows a group of buildings that follows the irregular perimeter of its site. In plan and elevation, the project is more reminiscent of collegiate architecture than of the solutions one has come to expect from SOM. It is certainly far removed from the institutional architecture of the modernist era, in which each function would have had its own building, open to fresh air and sunlight.

The Senior Housing Complex in Colton, California, by Joe Valerio is less inwardly oriented than Legge's design. Built on a nine-block grid, the buildings continue the fabric of the city. At the same time, the corridors connecting the individual apartment units form an enclosure with a small park in the center. In addition to the apartment buildings, which each take up a block, spread out over the complex are separate buildings for other functions such as administration, meetings, etc. I must say that some of the tower-like structures at places where the corridors cross a road look a bit like watch-towers to me.

Janet Rogatz managed to fit a whole institution, including offices, meeting rooms and dormitories into one three-flat-like building, and even make it accessible for wheelchairs. The result is an extremely compact arrangement in which the elevator, stairs and plumbing are all kept on one side of the building in order to allow as much space as possible for the remaining functions. The elevation drawing, however, does not allow us to judge the effect the wheelchair ramp and elevator shaft might have on the proportions of the house.

159

Multi-Unit Residential

Diane Legge

This master plan for a residential treatment complex for children with emotional and behavioral disorders expands the existing facilities. It includes two residential buildings for 40 children in a home-like environment, a main floor dining hall with kitchen facilities, a private dining room and guest room on the floor above for family visits, a school house with classrooms and a gymnasium, and an administrative building containing conference rooms. Planning within each unit addresses both the child's need for privacy and the institution's requirement for constant supervision.

In deference to the residential neighborhood, the buildings have been connected around a central quadrangle which provides a contained playground for the children. Key elements in the design are an extremely limited budget, flexible spaces within each unit of the complex, and a safe and secure environment.

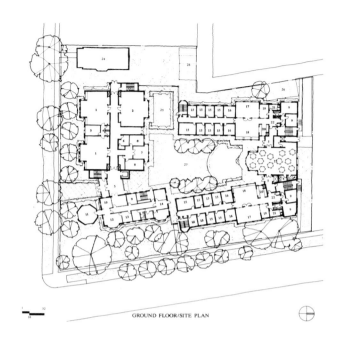

GROUND FLOOR/SITE PLAN

160

A design partner of Skidmore Owings & Merrill, Ms. Legge received a bachelor of arts from Stanford University in 1972, and a master of architecture from Princeton University in 1975. In 1988, she received the Illinois Chapter American Society of Landscape Architects Honor Award for the Riverfront Park at Quaker Tower. In 1986, she was included in the "Forty Under Forty" distinguished architects selected by the Architectural League of New York and Interiors *magazine. In 1985, she received a Chicago Chapter AIA Distinguished Building Award for the Boston Globe Plant in Billerica, Massachusetts, and a* Progressive Architecture *Award for her contribution to the Chicago Central Area plan.*

Her work has been published in Progressive Architecture, Interior Design, Interiors *and* Architecture *magazines, and has been exhibited at the Art Institute of Chicago, The Gallery of Design, and The Chicago Historical Society. Her work is currently included in a National AIA traveling exhibit, "That Exceptional One, Women in Architecture, 1888-1988," and "99 Chicago Architects," in Europe.*

Firm: Skidmore, Owings, and Merrill
Partners: Diane Legge, design partner; Robert Wesley, project partner; Peter Ellis, studio head

SOUTH ELEVATION SCHOOL BUILDING

EAST ELEVATION RESIDENTIAL UNITS

Staff: Peter Magill, Renee Sprogis-Marohn, and Joseph Pasquinelli

Anders Nereim

The sloping timber beams of this little apple barn suggest the sensibility of Deconstructionism, but they carry no heavy philosophical loads, just the prevailing winds. The barn is subdivided into a pair of interlocking vacation condominiums, each with a garage and three bedrooms. You arrive on the main (second) level through a stairway which is surrounded by a miniature building. It hides the stair and playfully shifts the scale of the space when you arrive, in response to the fact that you must duck under low beams to move around inside the unit. The upstairs is conceived as an abstract landscape of blue mountains, golden bolts of lightning, and purple clouds which suggest other things. Seeing Poussin's 'Landscape with Orion' may have set the stage for this.

Anders Nereim is a practicing architect and a visiting professor at the School of the Art Institute of Chicago. He has a degree from the University of Chicago, and graduated with honors and highest distinction in design from the University of Illinois at Chicago. In 1987 he was given a Young Architect Award by the Chicago Chapter of the AIA, and in 1989 he was named third alternate for the NEA Advanced Fellowship to the American Academy in Rome.

He has taught at the Universities of Pennsylvania, Wisconsin at Milwaukee, and Illinois at Urbana and Chicago, and has been a visiting critic or lecturer at Notre Dame, Harvard, USC, The Catholic University, the University of Texas at Arlington and Austin, and Kansas State University. He is a member of the National AIA Committee on Design and the Board of Directors of the Chicago Chapter AIA.

His work has won awards and has been exhibited in art galleries and museums internationally. His paintings and drawings are in the permanent collections of the Art Institute of Chicago, the Chicago Historical Society, the Deutsches Architekturmuseum, and the Chemical Bank of New York. He has written for several national magazines, has edited the Chicago Architectural Journal, *and was recently guest editor of* Inland Architect *magazine.*

162

Vacation Condominiums in an Orchard
Kenosha County, Wisconsin

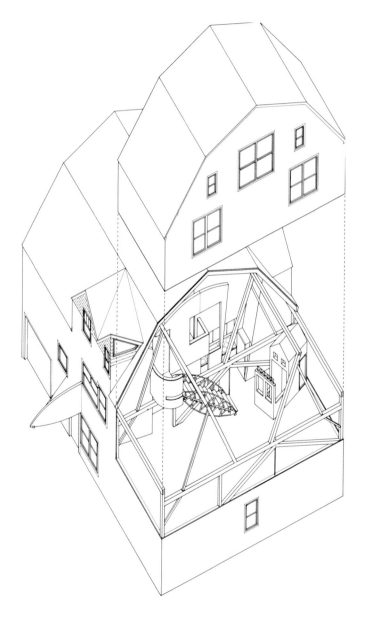

Firm: Anders Nereim Architects

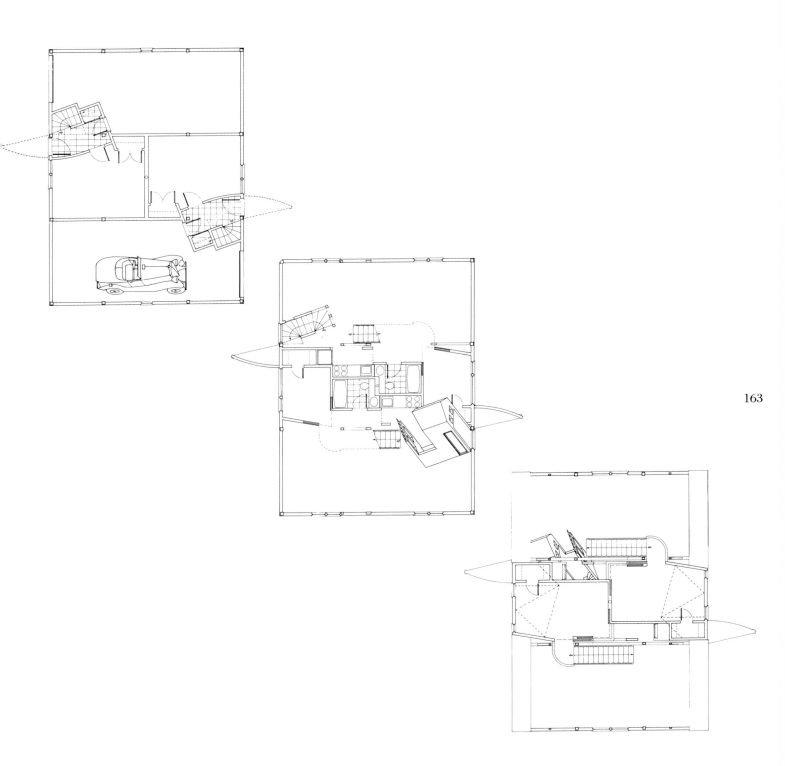

Janet Rogatz

Rainbow House / Arco Iris is Chicago's first completely accessible shelter; a 7,000 square foot temporary home for forty-two women and children who are survivors of family violence. It was created by remodeling a single family residence into a series of communal spaces, in which group and individual counseling, information, and advocacy programs can occur.

Janet Rogatz received her bachelor of arts in economics from the University of Illinois at Urbana, and her master of architecture from the University of Illinois at Chicago. She is a partner in Johnson, Rogatz, Wilson, Architects, and previously worked as a project architect, programmer, and designer for Dubin, Dubin, and Moutoussamy, and O'Donnell, Wicklund, Pigozzi and Peterson. She has written for various architectural publications, was the keynote speaker for conferences sponsored by the U.S. Department of Children and Family Services, and has exhibited her work in the Chicago Chapter AIA's Divine Details exhibit.

Rainbow House / Arco Iris
Chicago, Illinois

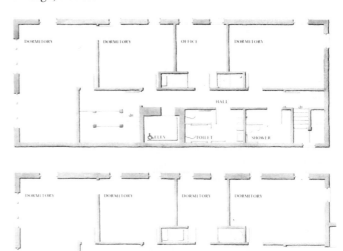

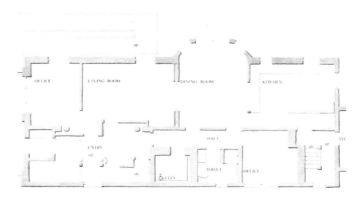

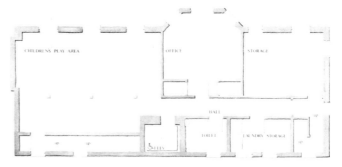

Firm: Johnson, Rogatz, and Wilson, Architects
Staff: Janet Rogatz, Karen Johnson, and Fred Wilson

165

EAST ELEVATION

David Swan

Kennicott Place is a residential development of twenty single family houses built in pairs and singly at the south-east corner of Woodlawn and 47th Street. They borrow their inspiration from the cottage vernacular, which can be seen throughout their neighborhood. Most of the visually rich examples of this style were built in the 1880's, but they still serve as excellent prototypes for today's mid-range housing market.

Kennicott Place recreates the feeling of a typical Kenwood street, with brick and shingled wood houses set behind a screen of trees and delicately detailed porches, similar to what can be seen today at 48th and Kimbark. All of these new houses will face a new private street off of Woodlawn Avenue. To maintain a non-uniform streetscape, each pair of houses will be a different unit type, painted in different colors, with a distinctively different front porch. Other forms of enrichment and differentiation will include bay windows, dormers, balconies, decorative exterior trim, and the option of building these houses in a mixture of brick and wood.

166

In private practice since 1973, David Swan received his bachelor of architecture in 1962, followed by a master of city planning from the Illinois Institute of Technology. He has worked for the City of Chicago Department of City Planning; Make & Associates, Japan; Loebl, Schlossman, Bennett & Dart; and Booth & Nagle. He was a visiting lecturer at the University in Auckland, New Zealand, during 1965.

His work has received a Distinguished Building Award from the Chicago Chapter AIA, and his photographs have been exhibited at the War Memorial Museum in Auckland.

Kennicott Place
Chicago, Illinois

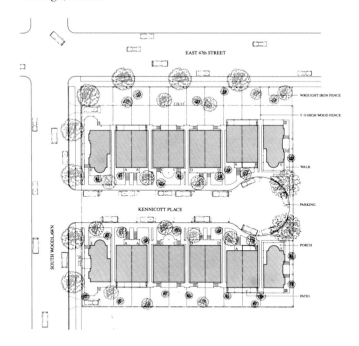

Firm: David Swan / Architect
Renderings: Rael Slutsky

Stanley Tigerman

Part of a large experimental housing project, the building has eighteen apartments distributed over six stories, with retail spaces located on the ground floor. It responds to the shifting angles of the sun so crucial to housing developments in Japan. The lobby provides the only access to a square central garden, which is open to the sky. The three apartments on each floor are reached by circumnavigating this central space. The effectively inaccessible garden is a metaphor for the garden of Eden, a nostalgically sought-after original marked as such by its white grid. The exterior black grid is a failed attempt to reconvene this original. Marked by gray ceramic tiles of different sizes, the apartments vary in their individual responses to function. Architecture's intrinsic optimism informs this design, but in the context of contemporary dislocative tendencies.

A principal in Tigerman McCurry, and a Fellow in the AIA, Mr. Tigerman received his architectural degrees from Yale University in 1960 and 1961. He has worked for George Fred Keck; Skidmore, Owings & Merrill, and Paul Rudolph. He has been a visiting professor at numerous universities, including Yale and Harvard, was the resident architect at the American Academy in Rome, and he received the Distinguished Service Award from the Chicago Chapter AIA. He is a Professor and Director of the School of Architecture at the University of Illinois in Chicago. He has written extensively for architectural journals, and is the author of several books, including Versus: An American Architect's Alternatives, *and* The Architecture of Exile, *which was nominated for the 1989 National Jewish Book Award. He is currently working on his next book, entitled* Failed Attempts at Healing an Irreparable Wound.

His work has received many design awards from the national and local AIA, as well as from Progressive Architecture *magazine, and it has been included in numerous exhibitions and professional journals. In 1988 he designed the installation for the Art Institute of Chicago's show 'Chicago Architecture: 1872-1922.' This year he curated and designed the installation for '99 Chicago Architects,' which opened at the Gulbenkian Foundation in Lisbon, Portugal, in May 1989.*

168

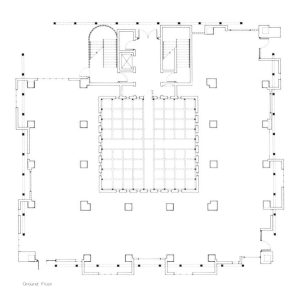

Ground Floor

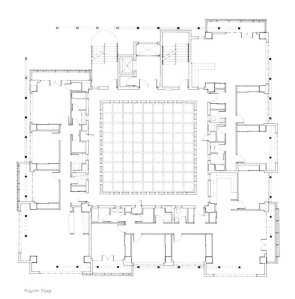

Fourth Floor

Firm: Tigerman McCurry
Staff: Stanley Tigerman with Paul Gates, assisted by Terry Surgan, Constantine Vasilios, and Roger Farris

169

In Chicago: Adam Koffman
In Fukuoka: The Zenitaka Corporation

Joseph M. Valerio

The site is at the center of the City of Colton, on the edge of Los Angeles. Single family homes seemingly inspired by Irving Gill or the Greene brothers dominate the area. The fabric and scale of this city, which calls itself the "Hub of Industry," is recalled by the scheme, which was chosen from 137 entries in a national competition. The organization is a nine-square, with each square a three story cluster of ten to twelve apartments. The center square is removed for the green. The fabric of the nine square is both extended, and carved away in places.

Opposite the Beaux Arts composition of Old Fleming Park, a palm court extends. The pattern is extended to meet open spaces by the reception hall and administration. To the north the nine-square is extended, but cut away to open toward the circular civic center built in the fifties. At many places on the site, the pattern of apartment clusters makes room for public buildings such as a meeting hall, a library, a crafts pavilion and the entry buildings. Any specific meanings of architectural language are purposefully lost, and the ambiguities of modernity are embraced, encouraging individual and unpredictable interpretations.

170

Joseph Valerio is head of Valerio Associates, founded in February 1988 with Randall Mattheis and David Jennerjahn. From 1970 to 1984 Mr. Valerio owned Chrysalis Corp. Architects in Los Angeles and then Milwaukee, Wisconsin. In 1985 he came to Chicago as design director of Swanke Hayden Connell Architects.

His work has received a National AIA honor award and numerous honor awards from the Wisconsin Society of Architects. He spoke in the "Emerging Voices" series of the Architectural League of New York and was selected to be part of the 1986 "Forty Under Forty." An Associate Professor at the University of Wisconsin at Milwaukee from 1972 to 1986, he has written books for the National Endowment for the Arts and the National Academy of Sciences.

Colton Senior Housing Complex
Colton, California

Staff: Joseph Valerio, David Jennerjahn, Brad Pausha, Randall Mattheis, Mark Klancic, and Brian Buczkowski.

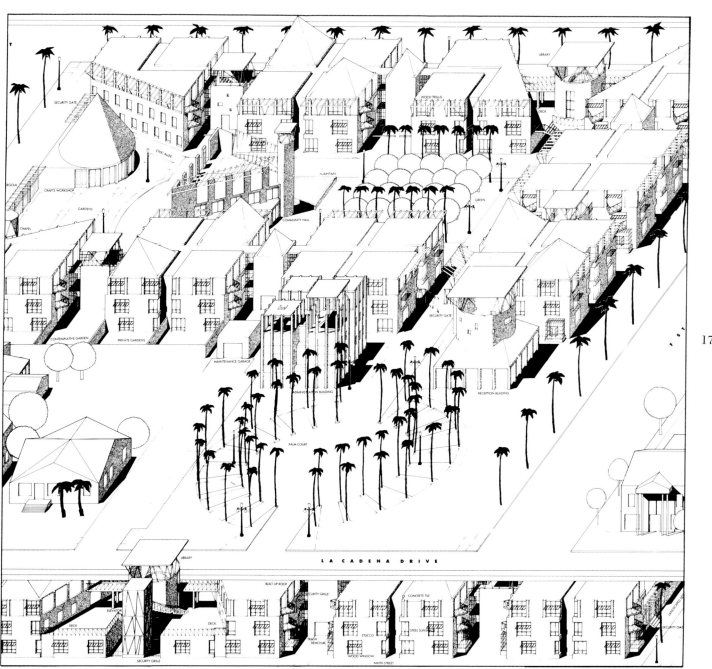

Dennis P. Doordan

This year's selection of large scale commercial work reflects the diversity of the contemporary architectural scene. This is hardly surprising; what may surprise some is the enduring vitality of imagery rooted in early twentieth century modernist design. The pioneers of modern design placed the relationship between architectural form and industrial technology squarely in the forefront of their efforts to develop an architecture appropriate for modern times. Recently, critics have assailed the modernist dependence on technology-based form and, proposed instead conceptual schemes based on models of literary analysis or linguistics. Today, however, when advances in medical technology compel us to redefine fundamental human experiences such as birth and death, and communications technology places the global village literally at our fingertips, it should come as no surprise that architects are still drawn to the expressive possibilities of contemporary technology. The antennae, masts, faceted crowns, long spans, and sophisticated skins that figure so prominently in this year's selection testify to the continuing appeal of hi-tech imagery and demonstrate the ability of architects to evolve new possibilities from the heritage of early modern design.

172

"Early" is the crucial qualifier in this discussion. Following the Second World War, designers of commercial high rises tended to wrap an austere, uniform, and relatively smooth metal and glass skin around slab-like forms regardless of the complexity of the spaces or the program. The homogeneity and consistency of architectural form, from small details to massing, was equated with America's technological sophistication and rationality. The highly articulated tall buildings included here indicate that architects are reconsidering that equation, and returning to the more dramatic architectural expressions of the first third of the century.

The complex massing and calculated asymmetries of Ralph Johnson's 100 North Riverside Plaza, for example, express the parts of the program without succumbing to the sophistries often associated with the dictum form follows function. Johnson worked within the parameters of the riverfront site and accommodated the program without letting either become a substitute for bold architecture.

Phillip Castillo's Singapore office tower and Helmut Jahn's Victoria Competition entry for West Berlin revel in the expressive power of the paraphernalia associated with modern communications and evoke images of constructivist experiments of the 1920s. The revelation of structural frames is another distinguishing feature of these two tall office buildings. Both architects assert that their towers play a positive role in reinforcing the urban orientation and metropolitan identities of Singapore and West Berlin.

Any doubts about the demise of the glass slab with the "fifties flat-top" are dispelled by three buildings from the office of Skidmore, Owings & Merrill. Adrian Smith's Dearborn Tower, Joseph Gonzalez's One North Franklin, and Peter Ellis's Phase II AT&T Center all sport sculpted tops that individualize each tower. The crystalline crown of Dearborn Tower, soaring 1,200 feet above Dearborn and Adams, may seem like the fulfillment of Bruno Taut's expressionist dream of architecture-as-Stadtkrone. It is only the formal properties of early modern design, invigorated with the romantic excitement of American Deco skyscrapers of the 1920's and 30's, and not the utopian content of the early Modern Movement that survives. These S.O.M. projects are not the fabled towers of an expressionist utopia, but the pillars of a dense, new, and radically transformed Chicago skyline.

The articulated surfaces of these buildings merit attention, as well as their tops and massing, for it is on these surfaces of granite, cast-stone, steel, and glass that the transition from the urban scale of the skyline to the pedestrian scale of the street occurs, and the process of self-explanation begins. The modern tall building is not too big to be understood, and therefore an alien — and alienating — presence in the city. Far too often, however, it is mute and unable to express itself in any but the crudest of quantitative terms. Detailing a curtain wall to reveal, either literally or metaphorically, the tectonic qualities of materials and systems figures prominently in many of these schemes. It is at this level of detailing that one still encounters claims of "the honest expression" of materials and technology and "fidelity" to a Chicago skin-and-bones tradition.

Laurence Booth's submission is one of the few projects to call upon the Chicago tradition in a more direct way. With "A Short Office Building Artistically Considered", Booth evokes the memory of Louis Sullivan's famous description of the prototypical tall building of an earlier era. Booth summons up no formal model, but a model of a critical position for the architectural profession. In place of Sullivan's concern with esthetic character of the tall building, Booth focuses on the environmental quality of urban centers. He maintains that the sky can no longer be glibly accepted as the limit, and he proposes the short (30-35 stories) office building as a prototypical solution to the problem of balancing commercial, environmental, and human needs. It is his project's strength that a survey of responses to it would furnish a telling index of the critical positions of contemporary architects, and with that the future of Chicago's built environment.

Rene Steevensz addresses issues of street scale and skyline presence in his design for a 28 story building on North St. Clair Street. Through the provision of an arcade at street level, attention to materials and surface patterns, and a roofscape inspired by the nearby Allerton Towers, Steevensz argues that new construction need not clash with the existing urban fabric.

The equation of large office programs with tall office buildings is no longer as inevitable as it once was. John Bowman's design for the Ameritech Center in Hoffman Estates and Dirk Lohan's McDonald's Office Building in Oak Brook are typical of the kind of corporate campus project in which the architect designs large-scale multi-phased development for suburban or (previously) rural sites. The programs for these developments may be written in the language of square footage and clear spans but the theme of the office campus reflects the client's desire for a particular kind of corporate environment and image. In projects such as these the architects are asked to realize the modernist dream of accommodating the machine (the computer) in the garden (the suburban campus or estate). Establishing an architectural character of "friendly informality" for a corporate environment "in harmony with nature" as Bowman and Lohan have attempted to do requires far more than merely providing economical and flexible structures with adequate parking.

William Ketcham and Richard Potokar also sought appropriate imagery in their projects, imagery that begins, once again, where the quantitative terms of the program leave off. For a German-based international firm involved in the manufacture of precision instrumentation, Ketcham provided a sophisticated exterior skin that reflects the attention to detail and exactitude associated with the Heidenhain Corporation. Pizzazz, not precision, figures in Richard Potokar's proposal for speculative commercial buildings in Fort Lauderdale, Florida. His point of departure was the Deco vernacular of South Florida; his goal, to evoke a distinctive sense of the locale.

Keith Olsen confronted special circumstances in his commission for the regional center of an international consulting firm. The Hewitt Associates site in Rowayton, Connecticut, included a turn-of-the-century manor house. While the juxtaposition of contemporary architecture and natural site features is often an effective design strategy, here the presence of a landmark added a different and potentially jarring note to standard solutions. Olsen responded with a design that defers to the manor house in terms of siting, scale elements and texture, yet maintains a strong contemporary identity.

173

While the machine in the corporate garden is the computer and the garden shed is a sleek, sophisticated box, a different kind of machine continues to demand our attention on the edge of metropolitan centers: the transportation machine. James Nagle's new Greyhound Bus Terminal here in Chicago and Martin Wolf's Consolidated Terminal at New York's JFK airport solve difficult planning problems with structural systems of expressive power. As these two dramatic architectural images demonstrate, perhaps no where else is the modernist dream of the integration of engineering and architecture, and of technological rationality and the power of expressive form, so completely achieved as in transportation facilities.

Tall and Office Buildings

Laurence Booth

At the time when tall buildings became poetic, they soared
only 15 to 20 stories. Today they commonly soar 60 to 100
stories, driven by the need for the larger floors which are
allowed by our generous zoning codes. These tall buildings
concentrate our cities, block the sun, crowd our streets, and
create dangerous winds for pedestrians. Shorter office
buildings would spread out our cities to the sunlight and ease
congestion. Sullivan focused our poetry on the "tall building,"
but now we suffer from "too-tall buildings."

In this office building project I investigated the poetics of the
"short office building" of 30-35 stories, constructed of concrete
and sheathed in glass and granite, with wide windows and
multiple corner offices. It seeks to express the dignity of the
workplace, the straightforward and economical tradition of
Chicago, and American optimism.

174

*A principal of Booth/Hansen and Associates, he received degrees
from Stanford University in 1958 and from the Massachusetts
Institute of Technology in 1960. He was a principal of Booth
and Nagle from 1966 to 1977, and of Booth, Nagle and
Hartray from 1977 to 1980. He is a member of the Board of the
Museum of Contemporary Art, the Chicago Theater Group, a
Trustee of the Chicago Historical Society, and Secretary of the
Metropolitan Planning Council. He has taught at Harvard
University, and the University of Illinois at Chicago, and has
served on juries for the AIA, and the American Academy in
Rome.*

*His work has been shown in numerous exhibits including New
Chicago Architecture at the Museo di Castelvecchio in Verona,
the Art Institute of Chicago, and Window/Room/Furniture at the
Cooper Union. He has received numerous Distinguished
Building Awards from the AIA, awards for excellence from
Architectural Record and Progressive Architecture magazines,
and the Distinguished Service Award from the Chicago Chapter
AIA.*

A Short Office Building Artistically Considered
in Memory of Herbert M. Hodgman

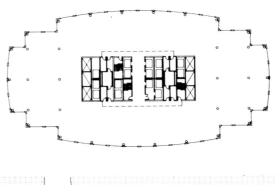

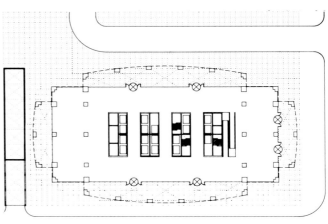

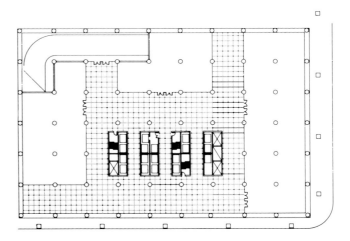

Firm: Booth / Hansen and Associates
Staff: Laurence Booth with
design principals Herb Hodgman and Dietmar Optiz

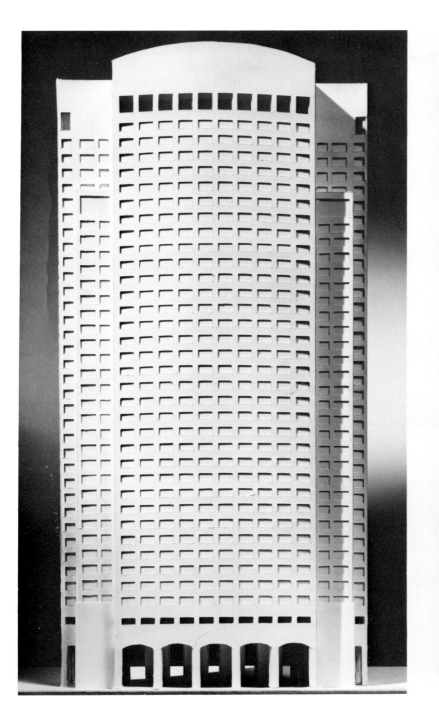

John Bowman

Jack Bowman, a principal at Lohan Associates, received a degree in Architectural Engineering from the University of Illinois, and a master of architecture from the Illinois Institute of Technology.

Working with Mies van der Rohe, he participated in the design of the U.S. Courthouse and Federal Center Office Building Complex in Chicago.

He was the project manager for the Martin Luther King Memorial Library in Washington D.C., and the project architect for the 666 North Lake Shore Drive remodeling, the 100 Park Plaza office building in Naperville, the Frito-Lay National Headquarters in Texas, and the Ameritech Center in Hoffman Estates. He was also the principal-in-charge of design of the new IBM Research Facility in Endicott, New York.

Ameritech Center
Hoffman Estates, Illinois

Our goal in designing the Ameritech Center was to create a stimulating corporate environment for Ameritech employees that would exist in harmony with nature, and accommodate the corporation's special needs and future growth. The first phase, a light-filled 1.3 million square foot office center, will house 3600 employees when completed in 1991. Situated on a 237 acre site, the four-story office complex will be 1,100 feet long, with a two-cross design that can easily accommodate additions. The crosses are formed by L-shaped office wings separated by skylit galleries which lead to a central skylit cafeteria. Employees will enter at the far ends on the third floor level, and traverse the length of galleries on suspended walkways, which lead to skylit atriums and ultimately to work spaces with ample natural light.

The building will have a steel structure and a highly articulated facade of varying shades of pink granite and rose colored glass. A rich marble-textured granite will be used above and below windows, and dark pink granite medallions will accent the paler granite used to clad the building's columns and spandrels.

176

Firm: Lohan Associates
Staff: Jack Bowman with Dirk Lohan,
Joe Caprile, Basil Souder and Dave Fleener

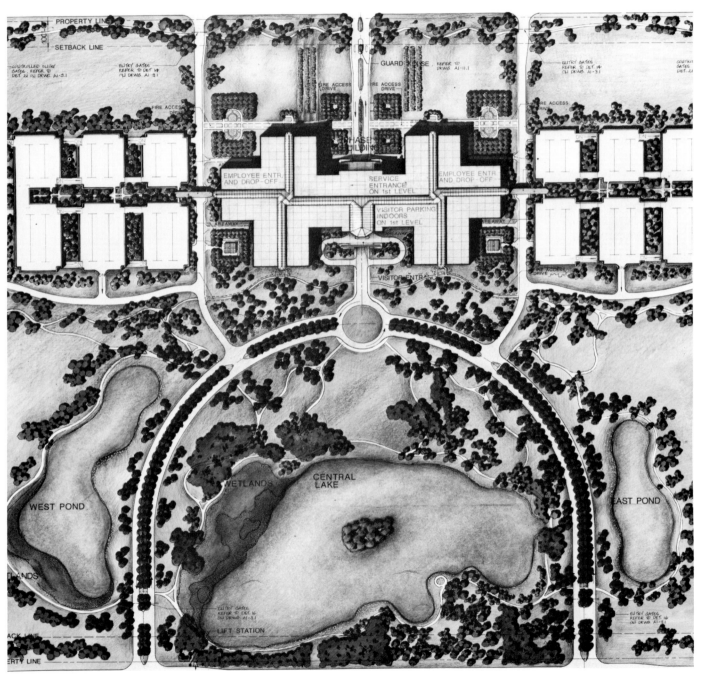

Phillip Castillo

Located at the historic Change Alley Arcade, this 36,000 square meter tower must work on two levels: the continuous urban context, and its identity on the skyline. Change Alley is a historic place to change money and purchase local handicrafts. The Arcade is now part of Singapore's ever growing financial district. The tower provides a gateway from the sea and Collyer Quey to Raffles Square, the financial district, and the other new towers in Singapore. It will have an identifiable image on the skyline from the roads to the city center, and from the various ferry and shipping lanes which converge on this tiny island.

The tower's shaft and podium are organized to reinforce the urban condition along Collyer Quey, while emphasizing the gateway to Raffles Square. The 30 story tower is rendered with a one-story frame and a set back at the 24th floor. A curving glass bay is juxtaposed with the background frame in order to control the scale and reinforce the orientation to the sea. The cool palate of white, gray, and blue are a welcome relief to the tropical atmosphere of Singapore.

178

A Senior Vice President with Murphy/Jahn, Phillip Castillo received a bachelor of architecture degree from the Illinois Institute of Technology in 1975. He worked for Booth and Nagle from 1975 to 1976 and for Hammond Beeby and Babka from 1976 to 1978.

Singapore Office Tower
Singapore

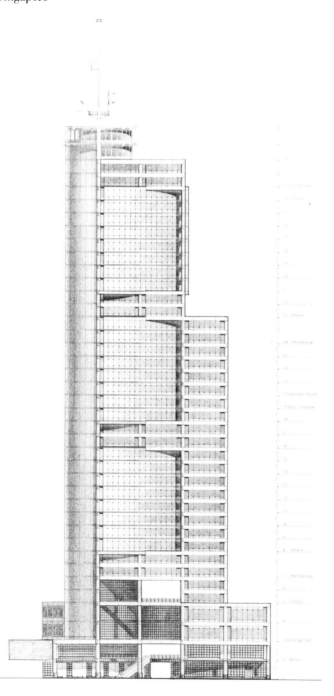

Firm: Murphy/Jahn

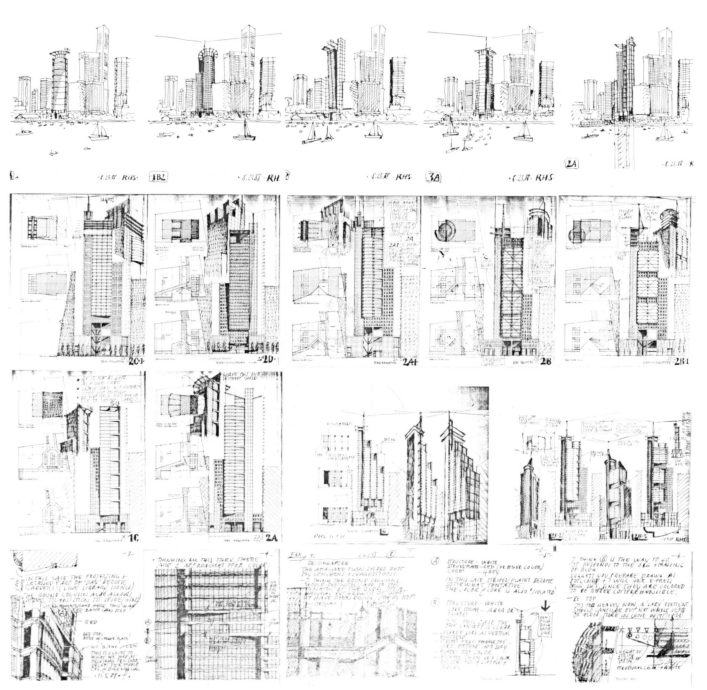

Peter G. Ellis

The AT& T Corporate Center includes the sixty story tower on the corner of Monroe & Franklin, now complete, and thirty-four story building to be built on the corner of Adams and Franklin Street. The two buildings had been planned together as a single composition during the initial AT&T competition in 1985.

The second phase building continues the sequence of public spaces established in the first phase, resulting in a pedestrian arcade linking Adams and Monroe Streets. The exterior expression of strong corners with two story punched windows, contrasting with vertical piers in the center bays, carries forward the theme established within the tower. The massive walls unfold to reveal a lighter glass and metal crown at the top.

180

An Associate Partner of Skidmore, Owings & Merrill, Mr. Ellis received a bachelor of architecture degree from Cornell University in 1971. He has been visiting critic at the University of Wisconsin at Milwaukee and at the University of Kentucky in Lexington, and has been a guest speaker and conducted seminars for the Kentucky Society of Architects, and for the College of Architecture at Cornell University.

He has also been responsible as studio head for the office building at 203 N. LaSalle Street, the Arthur Anderson Center for Professional Education in St. Charles, the Morgan Stanley International Headquarters in London, Dearborn Center, Chicago, and the renovation of the second-floor galleries of the Art Institute of Chicago.

AT& T Corporate Center Phase II
Chicago, Illinois

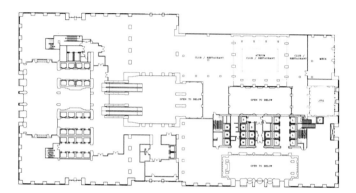

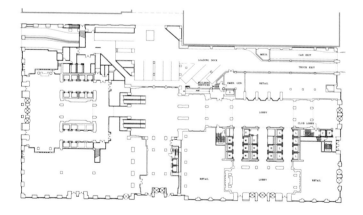

Firm: Skidmore, Owings & Merrill
Design: Peter Ellis, studio head; Adrian Smith, design partner; and Steve Hubbard, senior designer

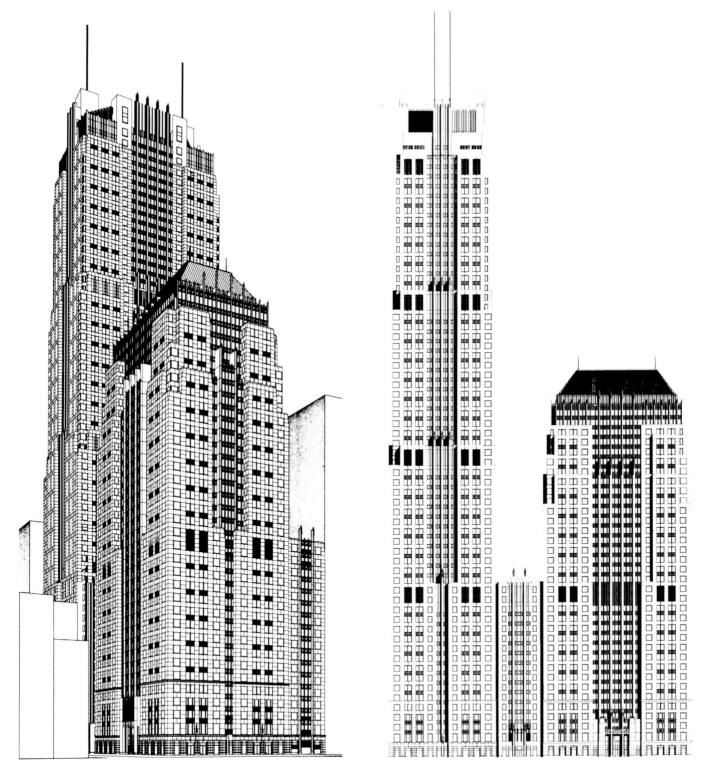

Management: Robert Wesley, project partner;
and Gene Schnair, project manager.

Joseph A. Gonzalez

One North Franklin is a building that metaphorically illustrates the way it is put together. It enriches the modern vocabulary without alluding to pre-modern methods of assembly or resorting to contrived expressions.

The cast-stone cladding is articulated to express the panels and their connective elements, making the assembly evident. The panels represent the building's parti conceptually as a pair of "bookends" in plan, expressed as tower elements in elevation, connected by a glass "link." The relationship of solid and transparent elements remains legible from the building scale down to the scale of the individual panel. The base of rainbow granite is flush, and doesn't attempt to advertise solidity through rustication or other allusions to thickness. Its thinness is revealed by metal returns at the corners, storefronts, and entrances. Like the cast-stone panels, the granite is expressed as a cladding material on a skeletal structure. In this sense, the building does continue the tradition of the Chicago School.

182

A design partner at Skidmore, Owings & Merrill, he received a bachelor of architecture degree from Oklahoma State University in 1973 and in 1988 he was named a Loeb Fellow at Harvard University. He has been a visiting professor of design and a guest lecturer at various American universities.

His studio won the competition for the Rowes Wharf project in Boston, and received a Progressive Architecture *design citation for the 303 West Madison building in Chicago. Recently, his Park East Housing Project in Milwaukee received a Citation for Excellence in Urban Design from the AIA. His work has received a Distinguished Building Award from the Chicago Chapter AIA, and has been exhibited at the Art Institute of Chicago, the Graham Foundation, and the 1985 Young Architects exhibit at the ArchiCenter.*

One North Franklin
Chicago, Illinois

Firm: Skidmore, Owings & Merrill
Staff: Gregory Beard, Peter Brinckerhoff, Michael Damore, Ricardo Fernandez, Joseph Hollingsworth, and John Shalapour.

Helmut Jahn

For twenty years Berlin attempted to find an acceptable plan for this important site, but keeping the existing buildings prevented the City from coming up with a solution which satisfied the planning issues and the image such a complex should have.

Our project combines space and object in a new typology. A stepped perimeter block surrounds a grand open space and is connected through large "gates" to the surrounding streets. It becomes a center for urban activities. Traditional Berlin elements, the perimeter block and the public square, achieve a new relationship. Given the envelope of this new urban type, we developed a new building typology for city offices which satisfies the need for natural light at each workplace, flexibility in layout and renting, and economy in construction and use, all through the incorporation of the latest technology.

184

President, CEO, and director of planning and design at Murphy Jahn, Helmut Jahn graduated from the Technische Hochschule, Munich. He was the Elliot Noyes visiting design critic at Harvard University and the Davenport visiting professor of Architectural Design, Yale University.

His work has received numerous national, regional, and local AIA awards. He has also received the Owens-Corning fiberglass Energy Conservation Award, the Brunner Memorial Prize from the American Academy and Institute of Arts and Letters, the French "Chevalier dans l'Ordre des Arts et Lettres", the R.S. Reynolds Memorial Award, and the Presidential Design Award.

He has been exhibited at the Venice Biennale, the Deutsches Architekturmuseum, Frankfurt, in 1984 and 1989, the Paris Art Center in 1987, and in "1989 GA International," Japan. Monographs have been published on his work, by Rizzoli, A + U, and the Paris Art Center.

Victoria Competition
Berlin, West Germany

Credit: Helmut Jahn, John Durbrow

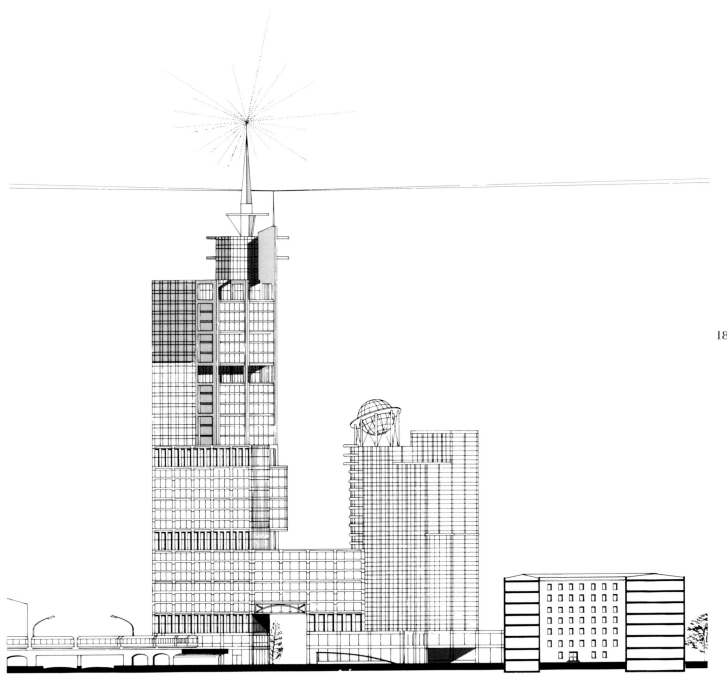

Ralph Johnson

A Vice President at Perkins & Will, Ralph Johnson received a bachelor of architecture from the University of Illinois, Urbana, in 1971 and a master of architecture from Harvard University in 1973. He has worked at Stanley Tigerman and Associates and has been a visiting critic and lecturer at the Universities of Tennessee, Wisconsin at Milwaukee, and Texas at Arlington.

His work has received a National AIA Award, a Chicago Chapter AIA Distinguished Building Award, a design award from Progressive Architecture *magazine, Honorable Mention in the Roosevelt Island Housing Competition, First Place in the Biscayne West Competition, and Honorable Mention in the Pahlavi National Library Competition.*

100 N. Riverside Plaza
Chicago, Illinois

This project is for a 37-story multi-use high-rise to be built on railroad air rights adjacent to the Chicago River. The program includes a lobby and street-level restaurant, a 500 car parking facility, a 250,000 square foot computer center and 500,000 square feet of rentable office space.

The massing and ground plan of the project reinforce the developing urban patterns of the riverfront. A public plaza and pedestrian arcade extend the riverside promenade which exists to the south. The massing of the building expresses the functions occurring within as simple rectilinear blocks, which are aligned in a north-south direction to extend the surrounding urban pattern. The river face of the project is given visual weight by the superimposition of a tower and a glazed loggia, and a big truss solves the structure at the south end, echoing the adjacent river bridges.

Firm: Perkins & Will
Design: Ralph Johnson, design officer; August Battaglia and Mark Romack, project designers

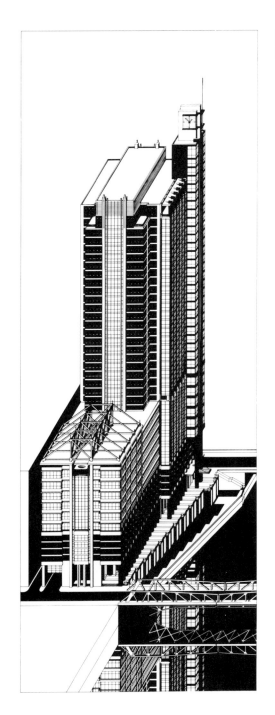

Management: James Allen, managing officer; Charles Anderson,
project manager; Joseph Pullara, technical coordinator

William F. Ketcham

Mr. Ketcham is a vice president and associate principal with Booth/Hansen & Associates. He received his bachelor of architecture from the University of Kentucky in 1974, and has worked for Harry Weese and Associates. He is on the board of directors of the Burnham Park Planning Board.

Heidenhain Office Building and Warehouse Renovation
Chicago, Illinois

Heidenhain owes its world-wide reputation to the manufacture of precision equipment and instrumentation such as linear scales, graduations, reticles, and more recently, electronic digital measuring equipment for machine tools. In 1889, a young mechanic named Wilhelm Heidenhain established a metal etching company in Berlin, which developed into the largest of its kind in Europe. After the loss of the Berlin plants in 1948, Dr. Johannes Heidenhain re-established the company in Traunreut, Bavaria. Today the facilities of Traunreut, Berlin, Chicago, and Sao Paulo have some 2,000 employees, 160 of whom are devoted to research and development.

188

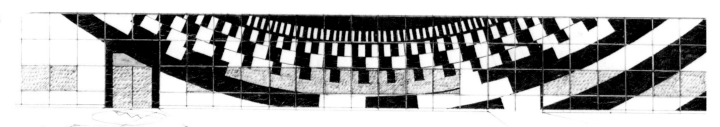

EAST ELEVATION - SCHEME D
1/8" = 1'-0"

Firm: Booth/Hansen & Associates

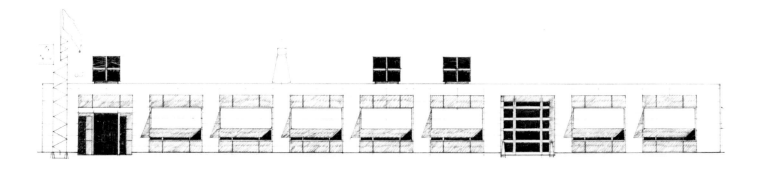

189

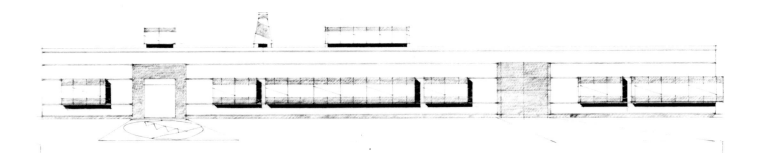

Dirk Lohan

The master plan for the Mcdonald's Office Campus is planned in phases for completion by the year 2000. The campus now includes a training facility, a hotel and the first phase of the office building located on an 81-acre wooded site in Oak Brook, Illinois. The newest addition to the campus is a 300,000 square-foot office building built over a 3-level, 740-car underground garage. The building is limited to three stories, the maximum height of adjacent oak trees, and establishes a character of friendly informality with a palette of natural materials, particularly stone, brick and wood.

The office area is an open plan where no one, not even senior management, works in an enclosed office. The building's structure was designed to accommodate the large open office bays without interference. A 30' x 48' post-tensioned concrete structural bay exists on each side of a circulation corridor. The circulation corridor is divided by a 12' wide lightwell on each floor which allows natural light to filter down from a skylight above.

190

A principal at Lohan Associates, Dirk Lohan graduated from the Technische Hochschule, Munich, Germany in 1962. He is a leading designer of cultural institutions, including the Oceanarium at the Shedd Aquarium, the campus master plan for the Field Museum, Adler Planetarium, and Shedd Aquarium, and continued work for DePaul University. He has lectured widely and written numerous publications on architecture and planning. His work has received Distinguished Building Awards from the Chicago Chapter AIA.

McDonald's Office Campus Office Building
Oak Brook, Illinois

Firm: Lohan Associates
Staff: Dirk Lohan, Joe Antunovich, Mike Vasilko and Gil Gorski.

James L. Nagle

The new Greyhound Bus Terminal on Chicago's west side replaces a 35-year old facility in the Loop. The first floor is devoted to passenger arrival and departure, operations offices, baggage handling and parcel shipping. Passenger areas include a skylit ticketing lobby, self service restaurant and a two-story landscaped lounge. Greyhound's Package Express is located on the north with a separate entrance and parking. On the second floor Greyhound's regional offices overlook the passenger lounge. The sawtooth perimeter of the second floor reduces solar heat gain and tempers the repetition of the cable structure when seen from the expressway.

192

Mr. Nagle received his bachelor of arts from Stanford University in 1959, a bachelor of architecture from the Massachusetts Institute of Technology in 1962, and a master of architecture from the GSD at Harvard in 1964. He has been a principal in the firm of Nagle, Hartray & Associates, Ltd. (formerly Booth, Nagle & Hartray) since 1966.

Mr. Nagle was chairman of the National AIA Committee on Design in 1981-1982, and he has taught and lectured extensively around the country. His designs have received many Distinguished Building Awards from the Chicago Chapter AIA, as well as several national AIA building and housing awards. His work has been published in such magazines as Architectural Record, Progressive Architecture, Architecture, *and* Inland Architect.

Greyhound Bus Terminal
Chicago, Illinois

Firm: Nagle, Hartray & Associates
Staff: James L. Nagle, Michael Messerle, Gintaras Lietuvninkas, Inna Goldman, d'Andre Willis, and Carl Gergits.

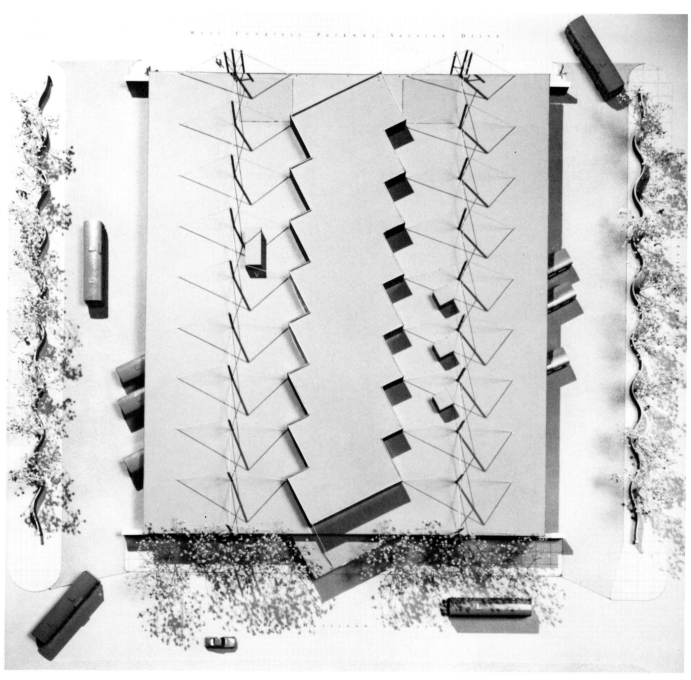

Structural Engineer: Cohen-Barreto-Marchartas
Construction: W.E . O'Neil Construction Co .
Renderer: James C . Smith

Keith Olsen

This project expands the office space, computer facilities and support areas for the eastern regional center of an international consulting firm. The building re-uses an existing 36,000 sq. ft. turn-of-the-century manor house located on 15 acres overlooking Long Island Sound. The existing structure is a landmark listed in the National Register of Historic Places. The 70,000 sq. ft. addition is placed respectfully adjacent to the mansion, allowing it to remain the focal point of the site. Two floors are arranged in wings around a central atrium that is the associates' entry to the new facility. Colored glass and granite are composed in a window wall that provides scale and texture while replicating in contemporary architectural terms the tudoresque style of the mansion.

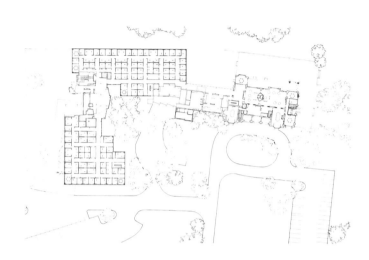

Hewitt Associates-Eastern Regional Center
Rowayton, Connecticut

A principal in Krueck & Olsen Architects, Keith Olsen received a bachelor of architecture from Illinois Institute of Technology in 1970. He has worked for C.F. Murphy Associates and was an associate at Hammond Beeby and Babka Associates.

His work in conjunction with Ronald Krueck has received numerous Chicago Chapter AIA awards, and a National Distinguished Building award in 1986. His work has been published and shown extensively in the U.S., Europe and Japan. In 1986 he was selected as one of "40 Under 40" architects by the Architectural League of New York.

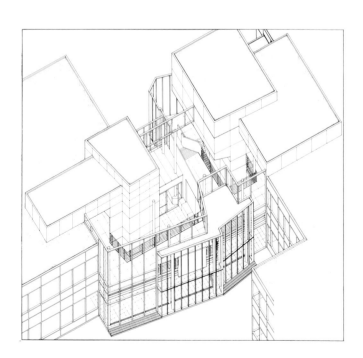

Firm: Krueck & Olsen, Architects

Richard Potokar

This project won a limited competition among six firms, by focusing on three distinct but similar styles for three office / research facilities. The three images refer in different ways to a local high-tech Deco vernacular, with the esthetic tone of the business park.

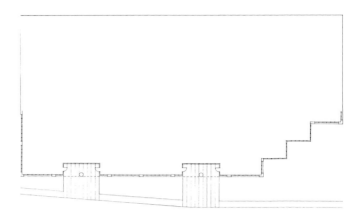

196

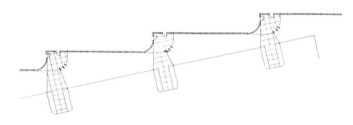

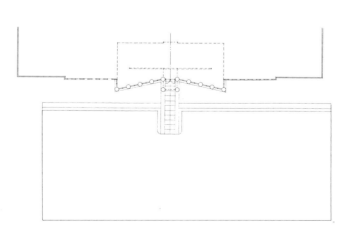

President of Richard A. M. Potokar Inc., Mr. Potokar received his bachelor of architecture from the University of Illinois at Chicago in 1974. He has worked at Hansen Lind Meyer, Perkins & Will, and Booth, Nagle, and Hartray. He won first place in the 1980 South Central Bell Telephone Headquarters National Competition, received an Interior Architecture citation in 1986 from the Chicago Chapter AIA, and was a finalist in the 1985 Chicago Bar Association "Young Architects" Awards.

Firm: Richard A. M. Potokar, Inc.

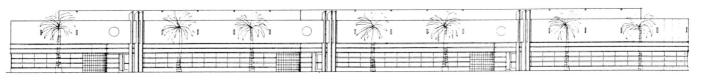

1

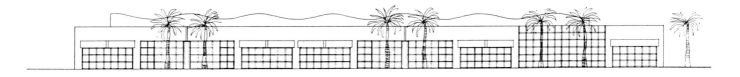

2

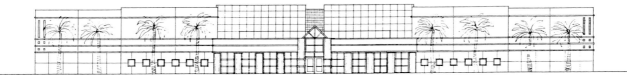

3

Adrian D. Smith

Rising to a height of 1,200 feet, the tower will be placed at the corner of Dearborn and Adams Streets, consistent with the concentration of office buildings along Dearborn Street. The five-story base occupies the entire site from Dearborn to State, in scale with the buildings across Adams Street and the stores on State Street. The base is conceived as part of an urban facade from which the tower emerges as a figure. The structure has a cruciform core of concrete shear walls, to which the perimeter structure is tied with two-story deep trusses at the mechanical floor levels. These are expressed as buttresses at the crown. A glass and stainless steel curtain-wall, with a strong vertical expression at the center of each elevation, allows the cruciform to read. The curtain-wall inflects away from the central figure in a series of sawtooth-like facets giving depth and density to the highly transparent skin. Detail is provided by ornamental spandrel panels in a hierarchical composition, with greater transparency at the corners, and greater density of detail at the center of each elevation.

198

A design partner at Skidmore, Owings & Merrill, and a Fellow of the AIA, he received a bachelor of architecture from the University of Illinois at Chicago in 1968.

His work has received two National AIA Honor awards, several Chicago Chapter AIA Distinguished Building Awards, the 1982 Interior Business Design Honor Award, and awards from Progressive Architecture *magazine. He has served on several AIA awards juries, and this year he was on the* Progressive Architecture *design awards jury.*

His projects have been published in Abitare, Architecture, Architectural Record, Architecture and Technology, Metropolitan Review, Progressive Architecture, Space Design, Interiors, Inland Architect, *the* AIA Annual of American Architecture, *and* Threshold. *His work has been exhibited at the Art Institute of Chicago, ArchiCenter, the Museum of Science and Industry, and at schools of architecture throughout the United States.*

Dearborn Tower
Chicago, Illinois

Firm: Skidmore, Owings & Merrill
Partners: Adrian Smith, design partner; Richard Tomlinson, project partner; Hal Iyengar, Structural Engineering Partner

Studio: Peter Ellis, Studio Head; Avram Lothan, Senior Designer;
Ernest Makkai, Senior Structural Engineer

Rene Steevensz

Rising from a three-story granite base, this 28-story building will be a focal point east of North Michigan Avenue. The scale of the arcade and the detailing of the horizontal and vertical planes of the base will give the lower spaces a human character. At the sidewalk level, the granite cladding conveys an image of elegance and solidarity which relates to the neighboring low-rise structures. The shaft consists of vertical and horizontal elements in a supergrid that defines the scale of the tower.

The building's height is accentuated by strong vertical lines of glass and granite which culminate in towers at the center and corners. The top is inspired by the Allerton Towers to the northwest of the site. These octagonally-faceted corners add richness and afford panoramic city-scape vistas for the executive suites.

200

Rene Steevensz is an associate and senior-designer with Loebl Schlossman and Hackl. He graduated from the Technische Hogeschool Delft, The Netherlands, in 1976, and has worked with offices in the Hague and Rotterdam. He taught at the Academy of Architecture in Rotterdam and the Technische Hogeschool Delft. His work was included in the 1983 Biennale "Young Dutch Architects" at the Berlage Beurs in Amsterdam. He has written for De Architekt *and* Wonen. T. A. B. K. *magazines.*

633 North St. Clair Street
Chicago, Illinois

Firm: Loebl Schlossman & Hackl
Staff: Don Hackl, John Schlossman, Rene Steevensz

Martin F. Wolf

A senior vice president and project architect for Murphy/Jahn, Mr. Wolf received a bachelor of architecture from Cornell University in 1975, where he won both the Eidlitz Traveling Fellowship and the Matthew A. Gaudio Memorial award. He has been a guest lecturer and critic at the University of Wisconsin at Milwaukee.

He was project architect for the United Airlines terminal complex, which received a National AIA honor award and the Reynolds Aluminum award.

Consolidated Terminal at JFK
New York, New York

This consolidated airline terminal at JFK is being developed jointly by American Airlines, Northwest Airlines, and the Port Authority of New York and New Jersey. It creates a new prototype for a combined domestic and international air transit station. The thirty-one gate facility inter-relates spaces for the departing passengers' sequence from ground transportation, and the arriving passengers' sequence from the aircraft, through customs to the arrival hall. The clear, efficient spatial and functional flow within the building is balanced on the airplane side with dual taxiways which ensure the expedient mating of aircraft to building. As a "port of entry" into New York City, which for centuries has been a gateway to the United States, the ticketing hall, arrival hall, concourses, and wintergardens, are an appropriate and significant innovation.

Firm: Murphy/Jahn
Staff: Martin Wolf with Helmut Jahn, design

September
Violated Perfection: Deconstructing Architecture
The top floor of the Graham Foundation was packed for the first meeting of the 1988-89 season, which was billed as a forum on deconstruction, also the subject of a recent exhibition at the Museum of Modern Art in New York. Organized by Stephen Wierzbowski, the panel included young architect/curator/author types who had originally conceived of the idea for the show, and other architects whose work could/should have been included in the exhibition. Several members of Chicago's growing legion of philosophical deconstructors were also present, but the architects's presentations were wisely innocent of the kind of conceptual pretension/confusion which causes a deconstructive feeding frenzy, and they escaped unscathed. Or so it may have seemed. In reality, Catherine Ingraham, the deconstructive gladiator on the panel, was practicing a form of intellectual Ju-jitsu on the architects, causing them to reveal the various personal sensibilities which inform their work. Michael Rotondi of Morphosis revealed that he first sets up axioms, or blatant assumptions, and then relies entirely on instinct. He said there was nothing conceptual about it, and the "disorder" in his work is just a reflection of a natural situation. At the end of the meeting, Dan Wheeler proposed that self-avowed "non-conceptual" architects, like Rotondi and Ron Krueck, are still very concerned with the possibility of achieving perfection. Krueck apparently is still striving to achieve it, but Rotondi is reacting to what he sees as the impossibility of achieving it.
—Anders Nereim

October
New Firms: Young Architects
This meeting featured the work of new firms, moderated by Andrew Metter. Presentations were made by Tannys Langdon and David Woodhouse, Joseph Valerio, Peter Landon, Dan Wheeler, and Karen Johnson, Janet Rogatz and Frederick Wilson. Langdon, Woodhouse, and Valerio showed one project each and were compelled to offer theoretical background. The remaining participants, however, gave broad overviews of their current work. Andy Metter and Joe Valerio challenged these participants, suggesting that their lack of theoretical discussion might indicate a paucity of ideas about architecture. Fred Wilson vigorously denied the charge and argued that the time constraints that had been imposed presented his firm with a dilemma: whether to show a single project with considerable elaboration or quick glimpses of their many projects. By choosing the latter strategy, they were able to show that their architecture was not about any single idea, but rather a number of still evolving ones. A close look at all of the work presented showed a strong interest in the theoretical nature of architecture. The current construction boom has led many new, small firms to think, build, and when the proper format is available, talk as well.
—Ed Keegan

November
Competitions and Winning: Selected Viewpoints and Discussion
This meeting of the Club engaged in a lively discussion and review under Jack Naughton's able direction of the two competitions for the Chicago Public Library. The Burnham Prize, awarded by the Club to Alan Armbrust, was for a proposal on the same site and for an abbreviated program as the recent international competition for the Harold Washington Library. The winner of that competition, Club member Thomas Beeby, and juror, Club member Professor David Van Zanten, related fascinating insights into the process and result of the competition from both sides of the matter. SOM's Adrian Smith added another voice from the competitors ranks. The emphasis on tactics for getting the job and for winning the Prize overshadowed more critical commentary on the nature of storage and access to a changing body of knowledge and information. Criteria for judgment, popular versus professional perceptions and the narrow constraints imposed on the problems satisfied the general curiosity about how things are done. Why they are done, and the alternatives that might change them are always more unsettling and less focussed.
—Sidney Robinson

December
Meet the Press
Anders Nereim, with admirable deft and grace, moderated an exuberant discussion of architectural journalism. Despite recalcitrant editors and hostile readers, the panel felt that there was growing interest in and concern for architecture. They discussed their varied roles as educators, advocates, and critics. Lisa Goff related her move from developer-deal-of-the- week stories to preservation consciousness-raising in the canyons of LaSalle. In a similar departure from the customary, Cynthia Davidson spoke of Inland Architect's unique emphasis on thoughtful analysis. Ed Zotti raised some of the most interesting and problematic questions. Having educated his YUPPIE, BUPPIE, DINK readership about the pitfalls of modernism, he (and presumably they) want to know why architects aren't more responsive to "practical" concerns (as opposed to the merely esthetic). But the E-word is apparently alive and well in the outrage-inspired writings of Paul Krieger who spoke to the need for architects to defend themselves against the (as yet) unreconstructed in Lisa's audience. Additional thoughtful commentary was provided by David Greenspan and Ed Keegan. Members and guests responded enthusiastically to the panel with their own provocative questions and insights.
—Linda Krause

January
New Museums in Chicago
January's meeting on museums focussed on the differing approaches of three projects. Coordinated by Wim de Wit, Curator of Architecture at the Chicago Historical Society, he compared the prestige of museum design with past religious architecture. Recent or proposed work at the Art Institute of Chicago, the Chicago Historical Society and the Motorola Museum was discussed by a museum professional and architect from each project. Katharine Lee, of the Art Institute, and Dennis Rupert discussed the Rice Building. Ellsworth Brown, Historical Society, and Gerald Horn analyzed their work. Sharon Darling, Director, and Laurence Booth presented the Motorola Museum. Lee presented the Rice Building as a well defined task, carefully studied and analyzed before engaging architects. Rupert emphasized organization and orientation in the new galleries and in relating to the existing museum. Initially the Historical Society perceived a problem in storing its rapidly expanding collections. Subsequently the problem of identity and imageability for the museum emerged as equal to storage. Horn saw a task similar to a laboratory building with distinct yet interrelated spaces. Horn wanted to make the building fun, to have its Clark Street facade continue the street's lively character, and once inside, to have the visitor encounter clear organization by using the existing museum as a basis of orientation. The Motorola Museum grew from the idea of the chairman of the company. Organized as any other research and development project in the company, Darling found that interpreting the history of the corporate culture of Motorola was as important as the history of the company's artifacts. Laurence Booth came to think that such an evolving collection should have visual immediacy, yielding a design permitting an initial, comprehensive and elevated view of the entire museum. Despite the technological content of the collections, the architecture is ecclesiastical.
—Kevin Harrington

February
Historians' Night
February saw many onslaughts, not the least of which was CAC meeting coach Sidney "Doc" Robinson's unleashing of a veritable tag-team of architectural historians bent on revenge. First we were ravished down to the mat by the power of "Deaf" Kurtich, whose seductive full screen images of de Monville's Desert de Retz were accompanied by his trademark knee-drop sound system, leaving us all in various states of submission. Next on the mat was "Hoaxer" Krause, who mystified us with the apparition of a purportedly archaeological exhibit by David Guize about several centuries worth of decoration for the Villa Bitrice, which never was. Confiding at the last minute that even she had not seen that which she was showing us, she disappeared exasperatingly into her own mirrors. David "The Humbler" Van Zanten next gave us another precise dose of his very effective stop-in-your-tracks Seyfarth formula, which unfailingly proves that quality work, done out of step, and with no fanfare, can still bring us to our knees. Kevin "The Harrier" followed, grasping that unnamed ligature between the Wright pectoral and the Richardsonian bulge, and ultimately delivering a mighty stretch to the imagination. The devastating "Wheaties" Bruegmann was last, as always putting his well-muscled finger on those tender spots in our recent history such as "Bad Taste." This time, however, he targeted our past visions of the computerized future, impassively delivered his punch lines, and left us in paroxysms of laughter.
—Anders Nereim

March
Accident and Order: Cities in Architectural Education
The weekend preceding the Tuesday club meeting saw architectural educators from across the nation converge on the Drake Hotel for the 77th Annual Association of Collegiate Schools of Architecture (ACSA) Meeting. The convention was an architectural marathon of white paper sessions, local tours, and position debates. Stanley Tigerman monitored the standoffs between such notables as Leon Krier, Peter Eisenman, Bruce Graham, and Thomas Beeby. The ACSA Convention's theme of Architectural Design and Pedagogy, along with many of its attendees, carried over into the club meeting, organized by Kevin Harrington. On this cold and windy night, the speakers seduced the audience with sun-baked travel slides, almost self-explaining the benefits of European architectural study. Norman Crowe described students in the University of Notre Dame's third-year Rome program learning that they were not the "free agents" they thought: they are really American suburbanites and part of a consumer society. The Rome program allows them to become "Freer agents," open to other values such as urbanism. Mark Keane, of the University of Illinois's Versailles program, put on a punk music video which collided multiple idiosyncratic urban images. Hub White, on a more localized subject, described the University of Illinois at Champaign-Urbana's new adjunct critic program as "one of the most interesting things that's happened to the school in the last three years." Many club members are participating in this program whereby a student brings his school project to Chicago for regular crits in the member's office. Presenters also included the Club's Burnham Prize winners: Gilbert Gorski, Tannys Langdon, Thomas Rajkovich, and Leslie Ventsch. They presented their work done at the American Academy in Rome, along with slides of their architectural discoveries. Each explained how the benefits derived from their sabbaticals contribute to their current practices. They passed on the following insights: Gil Gorski found it to be a "personal voyage of discovery." Tannys Langdon: "As architecture professors, we fight inculturation: students studying abroad discover alternatives to L-shaped suburban ranch houses." Tom Rajkovich: "Allegory and iconography were tools whereby you could create a continuum between past and present," which he illustrated with the Teatro di Marcello. Leslie Ventsch introduced us to Campo dei Fiori, where she marveled on the architecture of accident in a world of architectural order.
—Deborah Doyle

April
Landscape Architecture
"Where is Landscape Architecture in Chicago?" was the
question posed for the April Meeting by Robert Bruegmann,
the event's organizer. The speakers rose to this challenge by
presenting projects of such range and variety in terms of
scale, program and design intention to defy any attempt to
summarize. Ted Wolfe from SOM presented five very large
urban projects, all publicly accessible spaces included in
major private developments downtown. Mimi McBride
presented five very small projects, both public and private.
Two were particularly noteworthy: "L. A. Faults," was a
delightful private garden in Chicago featuring the "Richter
Scale" seat and the charming Prairie Avenue "Cemetery of
Houses," as Maria Whiteman, from the Park District and the
evening's official commentator, cleverly characterized it.
Professor Terry Harkness from the University of Illinois at
Champaign presented a very thoughtful theoretical project for
an airport in Champaign-Urbana: the "high-tech" intervention
in the prairie was designed to incorporate three narratives: a
settlement, an environmental wind, and a hydrology story.
The evening concluded with very generous remarks by Maria
Whiteman, followed by questions from the audience. Overall,
a delightful as well as instructive evening.
—Miriam Gusevich

May
Chicago in Berlin
John Syvertsen organized the meeting around the recent
Berlin Competition for an addition to the American Library.
Fifteen architects were invited to submit proposals; three
were from Chicago. Dirk Lohan set the stage with a
spellbinding description of growing up in Hitler's Germany,
the devastation of World War II, the Allied Occupation and
the symbolic importance of the American Library on axis
with Checkpoint Charlie. The post Chicago Public Library
Competition scheme developed by Lohan Associates was
intended to connect the existing 1950's library building (sited
as a monument in a park) back to the urban fabric of the
district. Lohan chose to obscure the "ugly" existing structure
by placing a simple and compact addition in front. They
elaborated the form by overlaying an exposed frame on the
facade, conceptually a projection of the original building
frame. The Florian Wierzbowski entry was described by
Stephen Wierzbowski as an expression of the contradictions
in West Berlin, "a walled city of freedom." Inverting this
reality, they inserted a wall inscribed with the names great
German and American authors to establish unity within the
elaborate composition. The sympathetic process of design was
described as pretending they were the original architects
weaving the fragments together through collision, diversity,
colors, images of 1950's futurism and symbols of the historic
airlift. Keith Olsen presented the Krueck and Olsen project
as a composition of pieces generated by their study of the
abstract forces inherent in the site and program. By
overlaying and carving into the existing structure using a
series of sensuous forms, materials and rhythms they
achieved a project of rich variety. The meeting concluded
with an open discussion and a review of the other entries
including the winning scheme by Stephen Holl.
—Garret Eakin

205

Index to Work by Members

Index to Work by Project Title

Credits

Photography

The Art Institute of Chicago ©1989	2, 10, 13, 15, 17, 19
Orlando Cabanban	8, 11, 90, 169, 175, 193
The Chicago Historical Society	36
Cable Studios, Inc.	73, 129
Bill Crofton	104, 105
The Graham Foundation	4
Hedrich-Blessing	60, 69, 198, 199
Hedrich-Blessing: Marco Lorenzetti	Cover, Section Dividers, 111
Hedrich-Blessing: Nick Merrick	190, 191
Hedrich-Blessing: Jon Miller	Front Cover Inset
Howard N. Kaplan	49, 152, 153
©Architectural Photography Inc.	
John Kimmich	143
Sadin Photo Group LTD	65
Steinkamp/Balogg Chicago©	89, 182
Michael Tropea	76, 77
Bruce Van Inwegan & Gregory Murphy	176, 177
The University of Wisconsin, Milwaukee:	21
School or Architecture & Urban Planning	

Acknowledgments

When the editorial committee determined to prepare this volume of the *Chicago Architectural Journal* in time for the celebration of the club's 10th anniversary, they realized that the volunteer work of the editorial staff could not be accomplished by a single editor working alone. When they made requests of their fellow members they were pleased that everyone responded positively.

The club is especially indebted to Cynthia Weese, who as president has done much to inspire and lead us all with skill, efficiency and good humor.

We wish to thank Rachel Garbow, editorial assistant, who learned that it is, occasionally, possible to serve three masters while retaining her sense of balance; Mary Woolover of the Art Institute; Hedrich-Blessing, whose color photograph graces our cover, and whose consideration helped our budget.

The cover is a detail of book matched circassian walnut in the stairhall of the Madlener House. The inset is the entrance to the house, which was designed by Richard Schmidt and Hugh Garden 1901-1902. It is now the headquarters of the Graham Foundation for Advanced Studies in the Fine Arts. The Chicago Architectural Club's monthly meetings are held here.

This book was typeset by Coman & Associates and printed by Walsworth Publishing Company, Inc.

Type: 10 point Bodoni Book with 12 leading
Cover Stock: 12 point Cornwall with matte film lamination
Text Stock: 70 lb. Mead Moistrite Matte